Pathologies
of the Self

To Patrick Casement, for his assistance during dark days long ago. Without his help I would not be here now.

Phil Mollon

Pathologies of the Self

Exploring Narcissistic and Borderline States of Mind

Published in 2020 by Confer Books, London

www.confer.uk.com

Registered office:
21 California, Martlesham, Woodbridge, Suffolk IP12 4DE, England

3 5 7 9 10 8 6 4

British Library Cataloguing in Publication Data. A catalogue record for this book is
available from the British Library.

ISBN: 978-1-913494-00-1 (paperback)
ISBN: 978-1-913494-01-8 (ebook)

Typeset in Berling by Bespoke Publishing Ltd.
Printed in the UK by Ashford Colour Press

Contents

PREFACE AND SUMMARY

For several decades of clinical practice, I have explored and pondered the nature and structure of human identity. This seems such a core aspect of what drives human beings – sometimes to gather together and sometimes to go to war. The simple and stark truth appears to be that we are collectively trapped in images. These may be images that we choose, that are given to us, or imposed on us – but they are all illusions, albeit seemingly necessary for our functioning in society, and we are inclined to defend them fiercely. They shape how we think, feel, and behave. In our narcissism we seek to preserve a positive, perhaps grandiose, image of self, engaging in slippage of logic and perception, as well as interpersonal manoeuvres to protect this. Sometimes we cruelly and sadistically enslave others to buttress our narcissistic image. Sometimes we have been deeply wounded by the narcissistic manoeuvres of others.

This combination of illusory image and coercion is well captured in the writings of the French psychoanalyst Jacques Lacan: "We regard narcissism as the central imaginary relation of interhuman relationships … seizing of the other in an image" (1956, pp. 92–93). Nevertheless, it is, as Kohut (1971) described, the transformation of these illusions that gives rise to core structures of the psyche.

A stable narcissistic structure provides some sanctuary from the pains and terrors of reality, and from the unspeakable horror of the fragmented self. Without this stabilising function, we have the chaos and instability of the borderline state.

Narcissistic and borderline states cannot be separated – they are two sides of the same coin. If we look at one side, we see the pathologies of the self; if we look at the other, we see the disturbances of relationships (both internal and external) and disorders of affect regulation. Sometimes one side is to the fore, and sometimes the other – and different authors focus on different sides. In this discussion, the emphasis is upon the developmental processes of narcissism since these concern the fundamental structures of the self, upon which all else depends.

Under favourable developmental circumstances, the components of our primitive narcissism are transmuted, via the empathic and supportive responses of caregivers, to form healthy structures of self, as revealed by Kohut's (1971, 1977, 1984) observations and insights. When these processes fail, we have the pathologies of both narcissism and borderline states. Human selves are indeed fragile.

All case examples presented here are composite fictions, comprised of elements inspired by many actual patients.

Narcissism, delusion, and the development of the structural self

"Everything I've ever done has been for your benefit," a narcissistic parent may remark to their child. Similar statements may be made in relation to marriages, employment, service to organisations, etc. The claim is that the speaker has been devoted to someone or something beyond any concern for self – that is, a claim to be completely lacking in narcissism! Such remarks may be stimulated by an earlier rebuke or criticism. What distinguishes the claim as narcissistic is, first, its completely unrealistic nature, and, second, the speaker's apparent belief in its truth. The narcissistic state is thus, in essence, one of delusion – a delusion about the speaker's inner nature. In more extreme instances, this extends to the perception of external reality.

As Roger Money-Kyrle stated:

> … *this narcissism … is a psychotic trait so pervasive in our species that to possess it is commonly considered to be not merely "normal" but essential to health … something the human race as a whole seems unable fully to outgrow. (1963, pp. 376–377)*

The narcissistic delusional state is not limited to those who appear overtly grandiose or mad in some way. It is commonplace among the population (even among psychoanalysts!).

All of us may, on occasion, slip into narcissistic modes of thinking and relating (or, rather, non-relating), but a key feature of the more determinedly narcissistic is the persistence of the subtle self-righteous delusion of personal goodness. By contrast, a less narcissistic person, when faced with a criticism, will be more likely to consider its possible truth, to feel some, perhaps temporary, diminishment of self-esteem, to ponder how the reality of a failing might be mitigated or repaired – or perhaps, after due consideration, decide the criticism is unjustified. In the mind of the narcissistic person, this process of self-examination is bypassed, and any possible injury to the grandiose self-image (which may be a mostly covert image) is repudiated. Reality is sacrificed to the maintenance of the self-image.

This is a key feature of the thought processes of the narcissistic person. Assertions and conclusions are made not on the basis of reality but on what serves either the person's desires or self-image. Truth is regarded as subjective, varying according to the needs of the moment – although the speaker might claim otherwise. In the narcissistic state of mind, perceptual and cognitive processes are distorted, through selective attention and inattention and slippage of logic, such that reality is subordinated to the privileged task of preserving a grandiose self-image. A milder form occurs when it is not so much a grandiose self-image per se that is preserved but a preferred perspective, world view, or belief system. The more malign forms of narcissism involve the coercive recruitment of others in support of the delusional image or belief. This can involve intrusive attempts to take control of the mind of the other (Stark, 2007).

Narcissistic modes of thought are readily observable among some of our more prominent politicians (Coffman, 2017). I will not name them, as they will easily be identifiable by the reader. They are often rather popular and seen as likeable characters – reflecting the perennial appeal of those who appear to have managed to preserve narcissistic illusions that the rest of us have largely, albeit reluctantly, abandoned (Freud, 1914c). Sometimes, they manage to seduce us (temporarily) into believing their own illusions. A notable tell-tale feature is the capacity for an essentially childlike slippage of logic combined with a counter-attack of displacement when challenged on a difficult subject – all in the service of preserving their private and public grandiose self-image. With some people of quick intelligence, this kind of logical sleight of hand is automatic and immediate, and no doubt seduces their own conscious mind as well as their audience.

Narcissism is also of course a marked feature of young children, whose modes of thought and grandiose fantasies are often wildly at odds with reality. During optimum development, the grandiosity and fantastical thinking gradually give way to a greater accommodation of reality. As Freud (1911b) observed, the pleasure principle is gradually replaced by the reality principle – although never completely, and not at all during dreams. When sick, or under great stress or traumatic suffering, our narcissism returns. And some children, such as those with ADHD, may experience greater than normal difficulty in relinquishing grandiose narcissism, which has a drive-like quality that can be hard to restrain when the frontal lobes are not functioning efficiently (Mollon, 2015).

Freud (1914c) noted that a child's narcissism

can be appealing: "It seems very evident that another person's narcissism has a great attraction for those who have renounced part of their own narcissism and are in search of object love. The charm of a child lies to a great extent in his narcissism, his self-contentment and inaccessibility." He observed that parents bestow their relinquished narcissism upon the child, who "shall have a better time than his parents ... Illness, death, renunciation of enjoyment, restrictions on his own will, shall not touch him; the laws of nature and of society shall be abrogated in his favour; he shall once more really be the centre and core of creation – 'His Majesty the Baby', as we once fancied ourselves" (p. 91).

Narcissism may be perpetuated also by social and cultural circumstances. For example, if a child grows up in a privileged environment, in terms of class, wealth, private education, and exposure to art and culture, all in ways that are at odds with the experiences of the general population, then the child's natural grandiosity and tendency to feel superior, entitled, and special will remain relatively unchallenged. The result is an adult who feels superior and entitled. This can be further exacerbated if the child is in other ways emotionally deprived, so that the illusion of social superiority provides a narcissistic sanctuary against the pain of separation and rejection. Again, this phenomenon can be observed quite readily among certain well-known politicians.

Narcissism is clearly a normal feature of human development, along with egocentrism. By contrast, there are perhaps three overlapping and interwoven forms of *narcissistic illness*. One consists of egocentricity and a sense of entitlement combined with active attempts to distort reality and to coerce others into supporting a delusional belief (in one's goodness, rightness, superiority, intelligence, entitlement, etc). Another, elaborated extensively in the work of Heinz Kohut, involves deficits in the structuring of the self. The third is to do with the myriad forms of defensive retreat from relatedness to others (usually because of profound early wounds to the structure, autonomy, and esteem of the self).

SOCIAL AND POLITICAL NARCISSISM

It is not difficult to discern the same narcissistic
phenomena that are found in individuals at the
level of social movements (Freud, 1921c). An idea,
a cause, a slogan, or motif, is selected as a basis
for identification and idealisation. The individual then feels part of a group through the process
noted by Freud: "[A] primary group of this kind
is a number of individuals who have put one and
the same object in place of their ego ideal and
have consequently identified themselves with one
another in their ego" (1921c, p. 116). The group
is idealised – perhaps for its moral superiority –
and this is how the Nazi movement perceived
itself, organised around an ideal of sacrifice for the
group (Koenigsberg, 2009). The "idea" is seen as a
solution, perhaps an urgently necessary solution,
to complex societal problems. Reality and logic
are systematically distorted to fit this delusional
simplification of complex issues. A further crucial
component is often, but not always, the presence

of a charismatic leader, who is able to argue the simplistic idea with emotional force. The idea, the group, and the leader(s) are all idealised. Like grandiosity, idealisation inherently involves distortion of reality. By participating in the group and identifying with it, the individual basks in the reflected glory of its idealisation and grandiosity, along with the euphoria of the sense of comradeship and surrender to the group mind.

Once the narcissistic movement has coalesced around its overvalued idea, the group and its members no longer care about the reality of their impact on others – since reality itself has been partly discarded. Members of such a group may not appear delusional because their distorted perceptions and compromised cognition are shared by others. It is the group as a whole that is delusional. As Freud notes (drawing on the work of Le Bon):

> ... *groups have never thirsted after truth.*
> *They demand illusions, and cannot do*
> *without them. They constantly give what*

*is unreal precedence over what is real; they
are almost as strongly influenced by what
is untrue as by what is true. They have an
evident tendency not to distinguish between
the two. (1921c, p. 80)*

Common to such movements are demands for societal or political changes that are, in reality, likely to bring about economic collapse. Proponents may argue that their "cause" is more important than the economy. The distortion of perception consists of the failure to recognise that we live in complex and interconnected societies, and that all the structures and functions of these rest upon a functioning economy. If the economy were to collapse, then all social order would collapse – nothing would work – and the population would be at the mercy of gangsters, brigands, warlords, and feral creatures of all kinds. There is a failure to recognise that social order is fragile, requires vigilant care, and can rapidly be swept away.

Like the individual narcissist, the narcissism

of social movements is blind to the subjectivity of others. It does not matter who is hurt or suffers as a result of the pursuit of the selected idea.

An individual narcissist may construct a grandiose self around a valid core of genuine talent, intelligence, or skill. Similarly, narcissistic social movements may seize upon a legitimate social, environmental, or political issue – but it is the dogmatism and selective inattention to the wider context or reality that reveals the narcissism. Skilful political demagogues will exploit and fuel the narcissistic injuries of the population, the wounded "national pride", and feelings of deprivation and envy, and then offer the false narcissistic solution – promising greatness.

Both individual and social narcissism can be profoundly destructive. Both heedlessly cause damage to others and to our collective structures and functions, through their idealisation of either self or a group idea. These malign phenomena are not limited to any particular political grouping, but can be found on both right and left, can be based on idealised forms of religion, and may occur among campaigners for all manner of causes. They seem increasingly prevalent, perhaps because the problems we face collectively are so severe and complex and can make us feel helpless and hopeless. Narcissism offers false solutions and makes the original problems much worse.

KOHUT AND THE SEPARATE LINES OF DEVELOPMENT OF NARCISSISM

The Chicago-based psychoanalyst Heinz Kohut arrived at the highly innovative perspective that narcissism is not fundamentally a juxtaposition to love of others ("object relations"), but follows its own developmental trajectory. In his 1966 paper "Forms and Transformations of Narcissism" and subsequent books (1971, 1977, 1984), Kohut drew attention to the two separate lines of development of narcissism: the grandiose self, and the idealised other/object. In the line of development of idealisation, the designated object of idealisation is seen as embodying perfection, of strength, intellect, beauty, or wisdom – while the self is felt to be part of, or linked to, this admired figure. In the grandiose self position, the formula is "Look at me, I am wonderful!", whereas in the line of idealisation, the primitive formula is "You are wonderful, and I am part of you!" The line of idealisation may be considered an intermediate position, between primitive grandiosity and acceptance of reality – although Kohut did not appear to view it this way. For Kohut, these two lines of development each follow their own path, grandiosity gradually being transformed into realistic ambitions to be pursued on the basis of real work, whilst idealisation becomes transformed into persisting inner ideals and values. Traumatic narcissistic injuries (wounds to self-esteem and the sense of self), or undue narcissistic seductions (inappropriate encouragement of childhood grandiosity) can lead to disruptions of these two developmental lines of narcissism, resulting in persistence of unmodified primitive narcissistic grandiosity or idealisation.

The unmodified infantile narcissism may be repressed, but always threatening to break out in shameful and destabilising ways.

Kohut described how the derailed narcissistic lines of development may be reactivated when given appropriate conditions during later psychoanalytic therapy. When responded to with tact and empathy, the primitive narcissism undergoes tolerably dosed encounters with reality, allowing a process of "transmuting internalisation" to take place, resulting in the establishment of realistic ambitions and persisting ideals, forming for Kohut a key structure of the self. Many positive and wholesome qualities flow from the transformation of infantile narcissism – including a degree of psychic stability, creativity, wisdom, acceptance of the pains and limits of life, a capacity for wry humour, and a quality of greater depth in relationships with others (Kohut, 1971). Those whose artistic creativity is blocked by the destabilising and frightening persistence of untransformed primitive grandiosity become freer to manifest their talents appropriately.

Kohut's clinical examples abound with accounts of narcissistic vulnerability – people whose sense of self and self-esteem were fragile, easily collapsing. These were more the kind of patients whom Rosenfeld (1987) described as "thin skinned" (Bernardi & Eidlin, 2018), Shaw (2013) as "traumatised narcissists", and Perelberg (2003, 2004) as those presenting withdrawn and "empty space" states. On the other hand, Otto Kernberg (1975), writing at the same time as Kohut, referred to the much more unpleasant "thick skinned" types, whose pathology he described as based on a highly abnormal fusion of the images of the ideal self, the ideal other, and the actual self. For Kernberg, this was the pathological "grandiose self". It is such people who display to an extreme degree the potential for narcissistic delusion and narcissistically distorted thought. The pathological grandiose self may also be linked with criminality, violence, and psychopathy.

Unfortunately, and confusingly, Kohut and Kernberg both used the term "grandiose self" but referring to different phenomena. For Kohut it denoted a natural childhood position, while for Kernberg (1975) it meant a highly pathological structure that might require aggressive therapeutic confrontation (Bernstein, 2013). Kohut did use the term first.

Through an understanding of Kohut's work, it is possible to see how the very same constituents of pathological narcissism are also the building blocks and crucial components of a healthy psychological structure (Mollon, 2000, 2001a).

THE HEALTHY GRANDIOSE SELF AND IDEALISED OTHER – BUILDING BLOCKS OF THE STRUCTURAL SELF

Kohut pointed out that a degree of grandiosity is both natural and healthy in childhood, as is the capacity to idealise a parent, teacher, or imaginary figure. These are necessary embryonic components of later ambitions and ideals. The healthy human being is developmentally "pushed" by ambitions and "led" by ideals. Among those who feel satisfied by their later occupations in life, it is often possible to trace their current passions to early precursors, displaying a thematic continuity that has provided an organising coherence to their ambitions, ideals, and use of talents – these forming a triadic structure to the Self (Kohut, 1971, 1977).

A charming illustration of these processes was provided on a radio programme, as the well-known "Supervet", Professor Noel Fitzpatrick, described his childhood experiences that laid the foundations for his later career. He spoke of growing up on a farm in rural Ireland and, as a ten-year-old boy, his task was looking after and counting the sheep. One night he noticed a sheep was missing and went to search. On finding the sheep had fallen into a ditch while trying to give birth, he tried to pull it out, but found the lamb had died. His father had told him to look inside when a sheep had given birth because there might be another lamb, and there was. He managed to pull the live lamb out and clamber back up the bank, but he slipped and fell, and the lamb slithered down the steep bank into the ditch and drowned. Noel was desolate and in despair and wished he was wiser and stronger and could do more. Subsequently, he developed a desire to save all the lost and suffering animals in the world. He also established an imaginary ideal-ised figure called Vetman, who had enormous and magical powers that were used for the benefit of all. Vetman would "take all the waifs and strays and animals that no one wanted and he would take all the bits and pieces that society discarded, bits of wheelbarrows and tractors, and springs from engines, and he would make the animals bionic" and fly from the chestnut tree in the garden and roam the neighbourhood rescuing abandoned or injured animals, bringing them home to be healed. This fantasy, that combined both the core ambition (of saving animals and making reparation for the death of the lambs) and its associated idealisation, sustained the boy's healthy narcissism and self-es-teem during years of feeling somewhat lonely and undergoing periods of bullying at school. Later, he trained as a vet and did indeed devote his life to healing animals, developing innovative methods, and also to expressing his ideal of love for all living beings through the Humanimal Trust that he founded. In these ways, his early narcissistic fantasies were transmuted into mature and reality-based ambitions and real achievements (BBC Radio 4, *Saturday Live*, 16 February 2019).

More sombre illustrations of the role of ideals as structuring components of the Self were provided by Kohut (1990) in two examples from the Nazi era, of solitary martyrs who preserved the integrity of their inner self even at the expense of loss of their physical life. Franz Jaggerstatter was an Austrian peasant who refused to compromise his Christian ideals by serving in the German army, calmly going to the guillotine in 1943. Kohut presented Jaggerstatter's account of a dream in 1938 that prompted his decision not to serve in the army. He had dreamt that he saw a beautiful railway train which circled around a mountain. Both grown-ups and children were streaming towards the train –

but then he heard a voice saying: "This train is going to hell" (p. 139). Jaggerstatter reflected on his dream and concluded it represented the Nazi invasion and the movement that so many people were flocking to join. The Nazi movement and its symbols were themselves an extreme combination of grandiosity and idealisation, but of an evil nature.

Kohut (1990) described a similar dream of Sophie Scholl, a 19-year-old woman, who was part of a group called the White Rose, which actively opposed the Nazi regime in 1941 by distributing leaflets and posting notices. After she was arrested and knew she was facing execution the next day, she had the following dream, which she reported to her cell mate. She dreamt that she carried a child, dressed in a long white robe, to be baptised. The church was up a long pathway, and suddenly she came across a crevasse gaping in front of her. She just managed to place the child on the other side before falling into the depths. Sophie Scholl's own interpretation of her dream was that the child represented "our leading idea – it will live on and make its way to fulfilment despite obstacles" (p. 148).

These people managed to preserve the healthy structure of what Kohut (1990) sometimes termed their "nuclear self" of persisting ideals and ambitions. Many do not, developing instead "a person who, despite his smoothly adaptive surface behaviour, experiences a sense of inner shallowness and who gives to others an impression of artificiality" (p. 136). This can be the source of profound depression and desperation later in life, fuelling midlife crises and later total despair:

> *I believe that there is ... a specific point in the life curve of the self at which a final crucial test determines whether the previous development had failed or succeeded ... I am inclined to put the pivotal point ... to late middle age when, nearing the ultimate decline, we ask ourselves whether we have been true to our innermost design. This is the time of utmost hopelessness for some, of utter lethargy, of that depression without*

> *guilt and self-directed aggression, which*
> *overtakes those who feel they have failed*
> *and cannot remedy the failure in time and*
> *with the energies still at their disposal. The*
> *suicides of this period are not the expres-*
> *sion of a primitive superego, but a remedial*
> *act – the wish to wipe out the unbearable*
> *sense of mortification and nameless shame*
> *imposed by the ultimate recognition of a*
> *failure of all-encompassing magnitude.*
> *(Kohut, 1977, p. 241)*

Thus, a guiltless despair may follow the failure to fulfil the basic agenda of the nuclear self,
consisting of its enduring goals and values, but as
a *structure*, its potential break-up is experienced
as "disintegration anxiety". Kohut (1983) gives an
example, from a case he supervised, of how the
nature of this anxiety can be misunderstood. In
the context of discussion of termination, a patient
had a dream: there was a ship – at sea – although
the hull appeared held together, it was in great

danger because all the nuts and bolts had gone – the ship might fall apart. Kohut considered the dream expressed, in a visual metaphor, the structural state of the self. The analyst interpreted that the dream represented the patient's anxiety about the end of the analysis, when the safe shore of the treatment setting was no longer there. However, Kohut argued that (although broadly correct) the dream was not actually portraying the loss of the supportive figure of the analyst or of the setting – it was focused on the fear of the fragmentation of the self. It was what he called a "self-state dream". The point here is that an analysand's anxiety is not always about the relationship per se, but instead can be about the structural state of the self in the context of that relationship. This difference is important, albeit subtle and nuanced.

For Kohut, the role of the other is not always a matter of relationship, but in addition concerns the way in which the responsiveness of significant others helps develop and sustain a person's structural self. This comes about through supporting

the gradual transmuting of primitive grandiosity
and idealisation, enabling these to develop into
mature ambitions and sustained ideals.

THE SELFOBJECT – ITS POSITIVE AND NEGATIVE FORMS

An important and key concept that Kohut intro-
duced was that of the "selfobject". By this term he
denoted a *functional fusion* of the minds of two
people. Rather than a fusion of the images of self
and other, he meant that the capacity for empathically informed thought of one person (e.g., the
mother) is essential for the good functioning of
another person's mind (e.g., her child). Crucial-
ly, Kohut pointed out that we never completely
outgrow the need for selfobjects – we always need
the availability of empathic others, sometimes
more so at particular stages:

> *Our mother lifted us up and held us close*
> *when we were babies and thus enabled us*

to merge with her calmness and strength; she was an archaic idealised selfobject. A friend puts his arm around us or understandingly touches our shoulder, and we regain composure and strength; he is a mature selfobject for us now. (Kohut, 1983, p. 397)

Certain neurobiological temperaments, such as ADHD, have an enhanced need for selfobject responsiveness (Mollon, 2015). When the availability or good functioning of selfobjects fails, the child or adult may experience a state of mental disintegration, with great anxiety and rage – that is, disintegration anxiety and narcissistic rage (Kohut, 1971, 1972, 1977).

Repeatedly, Kohut emphasised that a purely "object relations" perspective fails to recognise that the anxiety of losing the other may sometimes be a dread of the annihilation of self that would ensue in the absence of the empathically responsive selfobject. He wrote of the horror of the loss of the selfobject "without which the self cannot continue to exist", and that "What leads to the human self's destruction … is its exposure to the coldness, the indifference of the nonhuman, the nonempathically responding world" (Kohut, 1984, pp. 17–18).

Much of Kohut's highly original work was concerned with the way in which the patient in psychoanalysis will, if allowed to do so, make use of the analyst as a selfobject to resurrect and continue developmental lines of narcissism and the structuring of the self that had been aborted in childhood. This process was described as the narcissistic or selfobject transference. Kohut (1971) gave two examples of "self-state dreams" illustrating the selfobject transference. In one, the patient is in a rocket, circling the globe, far away from the earth; he is nevertheless protected from an uncontrolled shooting off into space (psychosis) by the invisible pull of the earth. In the second, the patient is on a swing, flying forward and backward, higher and higher – yet there is never a danger of the patient flying off. Kohut explained that both dreams illustrate the selfobject transference protection against uncontrolled grandiose exhibitionist excitement.

The point about the selfobject is that at certain stages of development, and to some extent throughout life, our self-esteem and sense of personal cohesion and coherence are dependent on the attuned responsiveness of others. Drawing on Kohut's work and also that of attachment theorists, Schore (1994) outlined the neurobiological basis of the selfobject – which could also be framed as the "dyadic regulation of affect" by the "social brain".

THE MALIGN VARIANT OF THE SELFOBJECT

Although Kohut emphasised developmentally positive aspects of the selfobject, there are also developmentally malign variants. Some people, both children and adults, have a particular capacity to recruit others into functioning as selfobjects, to the extent that the other person ceases to function independently. In such instances, it is as if one person operates as a narcissistic agent, hijacking the other person's mind. The selfobject process has then advanced beyond the normal and healthy forms whereby one person provides emotional support to another, and has become a form of parasitic predation. It may be compared with similar processes denoted by Melanie Klein's (1946) concept of projective identification, which includes the fantasy of penetrating the body or mind of the other in order to exert control – but the interpersonal manoeuvres I am describing have a reality beyond that of fantasy. The most common relationship contexts in which this occurs are between mother and child and between sexual partners. It can be a subtle and insidious process, developing without the "target" person's conscious awareness. Beginning with selective rewards and reinforcements of behaviour that please the narcissistic agent, and punishment by aversive responses (cold withdrawal, shouting, rage, tantrums, appearing deeply wounded) of behaviour that displeases, the target person's mind and behaviour are brought under the agent's control. Physical violence may occur. This process of narcissistic grooming can be a core feature in the development of "coercive and controlling behaviour", which is now a crime in the UK (Stark, 2007; Home Office, 2015; Walby & Towers, 2018). It is clearly also a feature of predatory sexual "grooming gangs" who target vulnerable young women. However, it can also occur between a child and mother, where the child is the narcissistic agent who has possessed the mother's mind. Such examples may evoke feelings of horror and are frequently hidden because of extensive shame.

Sometimes it is the mother, or a tyrannical father, who acts as the narcissistic agent. The child's mind is possessed (Kohut, 1979). He or she then experiences a lack of autonomy, and perhaps guilt and anxiety over any independent thought or action. Sometimes this takes the form of what I have called "psychic murder syndrome" (Mollon, 2002), whereby the mother unconsciously works to "murder" the child's authentic self and replace it with a "replica" that is more in line with her image of

her ideal child – in a manner somewhat analogous
to the murder of women in the novel and film of
The Stepford Wives.

These are all ways in which narcissistic agents
drive others mad (Gear, Hill, & Liendo, 1981; Gear,
Liendo, & Scott, 1983) and seek to imprison them
in a position of subjugation (Shaw, 2013; Turco,
2014; Greenberg, 2016).

In his 1971 paper on narcissism and the death
instinct, Herbert Rosenfeld described the common
appearance of gangs and mafia-type figures and
organisations in certain deeply withdrawn patients,
whom he saw as trapped in very powerful and malign internal mental structures. These react with
threats and intimations of violence if the patient
speaks of them and reveals any of the internal secrets. Although possibly somewhat different from
the patients Rosenfeld was describing, similar
phenomena are extremely common among those
who are given a diagnosis of borderline personality
disorder (BPD) and who experience destructive
internal voices. It seems that both internal and

external mafias operate similarly, and both aim to force others to abandon independent thought and fall in line with the desires of the parasitic narcissistic agents – see also Kalshed's (1996) description of the malign internal self-care system that attacks the vulnerable self like a kind of psychic autoimmune disorder.

It appears that two broad categories of narcissistic disturbance may be distinguished here: (1) those who are narcissistic agents, recruiting others to support their grandiose and egocentric self; (2) those who are the victims of the narcissistic agents, who function as hosts to the narcissistic parasitism of the latter. Both agents and victims suffer from narcissistic vulnerability and disintegration anxiety. However, the agents react with rage and seek to coerce reality (other people) to fall in line to support their injured grandiosity. Shaw (2013) describes a similar distinction in terms of traumatising and traumatised narcissists, and explores its relevance to wider social movements, couple dynamics, and cults.

Between these two extremes of narcissistic

agents and victims, we have the myriad ways in which all of us face challenges to our narcissism throughout our lives. We all have to come to terms with painful reality, which includes recognising that others are of equal importance, may suffer as we do, and that life involves repeated disappointments and frustrations, and ultimately death. Some people develop psychotic delusions as a defence against unbearable reality. The narcissistic agents opt for a related but more hidden strategy – of recruiting other people, through seduction or threat, to shore up their potentially crumbling grandiosity and sense of self. In this way, they draw others, sometimes whole nations, into their madness.

It can be important to discern which form of narcissism predominates in any particular case. Rosenfeld (1987) noted that "thin skinned" narcissistically vulnerable patients may have been repeatedly traumatised in their self-esteem, and therefore "… one has to be particularly on guard not to add to these traumas by making mistakes in our analytic approach which humiliate such people and put them down. These mistakes are very difficult to remedy afterwards" (p. 275). One style of psychoanalysis, which is unfortunately still to be found, can be particularly damaging: "The analysis and the patient may be brought near to collapse … if the destructive aspects of a patient's behaviour are constantly repeated in the analyst's interpretations. Such patients can end the analysis very much worse off than before" (p. 274). As a result of his clinical observations, Rosenfeld's own style of analytic work changed over the years (Borgogno, 2016).

Of course, the narcissistic agent and the victim may sometimes be found within the same patient, each position predominating at different times, the agent within subjugating the victim within, such that the two parts of the personality system are locked in an endless sadomasochistic "prey–predator' dance (Mollon, 2015) – a complex and vacillating position presenting considerable challenges for the clinician. This is the case with the internal mafia organisations described by Rosenfeld in his earlier paper (1971), and the malign

voices experienced by many patients with psychotic and borderline conditions (Mollon, 1996).
Another example of this might be the patient described by Perelberg (2004) who reported a dream
in which he was God and there was a baby in a cot,
and in his position as God he was to decide whether the baby lived or died – the scenario changing so
that in one version the baby lived and in another it
died. This oscillating dynamic was also played out
in the transference, whereby either the patient or
the analyst would be in the position of the helpless
baby and the other would be the all-powerful God.

THE NARCISSISTIC AND REALITY POSITIONS

One way of conceptualising the differing ways of
responding to narcissistically wounding aspects of
reality is to consider two positions or constellations
of mental attitudes, that we may move in and out
of at different stages of life: the narcissistic position
and the reality position. These are analogous to
the paranoid-schizoid and depressive positions of

Melanie Klein (1946), which also describe varying modes of relating to painful aspects of reality – the paranoid-schizoid position being characterised by primitive defences such as splitting and projective identification, while the depressive position reflects a more integrated acceptance of "depressing" aspects of reality, such as loss, vulnerability, and ambivalence. In the narcissistic position, the person attempts to repudiate reality, strives to maintain an unrealistic grandiose self-image, persists in egocentricity, and regards others as unimportant except insofar as they serve his or her needs. The narcissistic position is based on a fundamental self-deception, and an attempt to coerce or seduce others into supporting this deception. By contrast, in the reality position, there is an acceptance of painful aspects of reality, a willingness to *suffer* narcissistic wounds, and a recognition of the inherent value of other people. There is a commitment to truth. Under stress, there is also the potential to slip back into the narcissistic position – which, in extreme circumstances, can become a psychosis.

The narcissistic vs reality positions

(analogous to the paranoid-schizoid and depressive positions)

Narcissistic position	Reality position
• Attempts to preserve grandiose self-image	• Accepts the impingement of reality upon the "grandiose self"
• Intolerance of narcissistic pain and shame	• Suffers narcissistic injuries – feels the narcissistic pain – accepts shame
• Manic denial of reality that is at odds with grandiose image	• Capacity for empathy – recognises "there are others who have the same needs and emotions as me" – recognises the other as *autonomous other*
• Egocentricity	
• Lack of empathy	
• Entitlement	• Appreciates that we have a responsibility to care for others as well as ourselves
• Lies, confabulation and self-delusion	
• Manipulative and exploitative stance	• Treats others with respect and truthfulness
	• Refrains from deluding self or others

The realm of the imaginary

In terms of Jacques Lacan's (2013) framework of the three registers, the imaginary, the symbolic, and the real, we might say that the narcissistically disturbed person is trapped in the imaginary, the realm of images of self. The real is repudiated, including the reality of other people as autonomous beings. The realm of the symbolic, which is based around the law, logic, and a separation of signifier and signified, is degraded – words and statements mean only what the speaker decides they mean.

The real and the symbolic are sacrificed in favour of the need to maintain the desired image of the self and its mirror in the eyes of the Other.

A necessary developmental achievement of early life is to distinguish and integrate, from an initially undifferentiated phenomenological world, the three registers of the imaginary, the symbolic, and the real. This means that the developing child comes to appreciate that there is the world of external reality, there is also a realm of imagery and fantasy, and there is a realm of words, symbols, and other cultural phenomena. Crucial to this development is a distinction between reality and fantasy, and also a recognition that words and language in general follow certain laws. Words do not mean exactly what the speaker decides they mean. To function in human society, these realms need to be both distinguished and integrated. The person needs to be able to find his or her place in society – a place with a name. This means that he or she can state their name, place of birth and current residence, occupation, educational level, and can provide a narrative history of their life – and that all these will be based in truth that is tied to reality. At the same time, the person will be able to make use of imagination and fantasy without ever confusing these with reality. For most people, these three registers evolve and integrate naturally over time. A young child, for example, will babble and play with sounds and words, and will not fully distinguish playful fantasy from reality. Gradually, a respect for the lawful use of language develops, involving grammar and consensual linking of signifier (words) and signified. For some, it seems, these registers do not develop in the normal way – even though the person may appear superficially "normal".

While passing as normal, there may be occasional indications of an underlying disorder of the registers. For example, the person may make an apparent statement of fact that appears entirely without empirical foundation – typically leaving the listener baffled and embarrassed, perhaps puzzling over whether the speaker had confused a dream with reality. In the consulting room, this may take the form of claiming that the analyst had made a particular remark, or had done a particular thing, or had been seen in a particular place – none of which had a basis in fact. Another indication might be that the speaker uses a word in a peculiarly idiosyncratic way that does not correspond to its consensual or dictionary meaning.

The narcissistic aspects of such a disorder are apparent insofar as the slippage of the registers is in the direction of maintaining a grandiose image of the self. In such instances, the person appears to retain a positive self-enhancing view of a situation that may be markedly at odds with that of others. This may be at times attractive to some, who may admire the person's remarkable self-confidence, and may feel some nostalgia for their own lost infantile narcissism. These narcissistic qualities may also propel a person to the top of organisations, in business, professional life, or politics – although the underlying narcissistic psychosis will often eventually become apparent.

In normal development, the young child

gradually arrives at realisations that the world is governed by laws – the laws of physics, for physical reality, and the human-made laws of language, culture, and the legal system. The Freudian "reality principle" comes to prevail over the earlier "pleasure principle", as the child gradually appreciates that fantasy is distinct from reality, that delayed gratification may be necessary for longer-term goals, and that human social conduct is subject to complex laws and conventions. In Lacan's writings, the function of representing the "law" is often seen as embodied by the father – hence Lacan's famous phrase "the law of the father", or "the name of the father". The father is seen as representing a boundary between mother and child – the primal law that says the child cannot possess the mother and the mother cannot eat her child. Of course, the function of the law is expressed in many other aspects of the child's early life, but problems do seem to arise if there is no one in the child's environment who represents the law. It is important that the father himself is seen as subject to the law. A particular difficulty can follow when the father behaves in such a way as to appear beyond the law.

While narcissistic manipulations of imagery are primarily intrapsychic processes, some are also buttressed interpersonally. This is seen starkly in those cases where one partner engages in coercive and controlling behaviour (Stark, 2007). Here, the narcissistic perpetrator takes control of the victim's mind in an insidious and cumulative way, forcing him or her to identify with a particular image. Restrictions are increasingly placed on the victim's freedom of action, by means of emotional and sometimes physical threats and inducement of guilt and shame. Gradually the person's self-esteem and self-image are degraded, becoming suffused with feelings of worthlessness and toxic shame. Most damaging of all can be the sense of being "nothing" outside the orbit of the narcissist. In this way, the aggressive narcissist manipulates reality interpersonally, recruiting the victim to embody the negative self-image, while he or she preserves the positive grandiose self. The narcissist requires a victim in order to maintain the grandiose self, but whilst in this state he or she believes in the inflated positive self-image. In more extreme instances, the narcissistic leader (e.g., a Hitler, or religious figure-head) requires the adoration of followers and the existence of denigrated others who embody the degraded self-image (e.g., Jewish people, or infidels, or other scapegoated groups). Such malign narcis-sistic personalities are characterised by a psychotic degree of certainty in their own rightness. The ca-pacity for self-doubt is a mark of sanity.

While the aggressive narcissist is engaged in a lifelong campaign to ward off the negative self-image and preserve a pathological grandiose self, often recruiting others to function as mirrors of the grandiose self or containers of the project-ed negative self, there is also a deeper danger. To be forced to identify with the negative self-image can certainly be deeply aversive, but an even more unbearable position is to feel there is no self-image, no identity, and no place in the symbolic register, no place in the world. It is the position of having no position – of having and being nothing to be seen or recognised. Leader (2012), following Lacan, notes that people with an underlying latent psychosis often become ill at times of change of their social position, such as marriage, retirement, divorce, loss of job, promotion at work or being overlooked for promotion, death of parents, etc. We might say that all the developmental challenges that require us to adapt to a change in our societal position are known to be triggers for psychosis – most notably late adolescence. These are all moments when a relatively safe cocoon of security and predictability of mirroring relationships is broken by a shift in the person's place in the social world. As Leader puts it, "[T]he symbolic network … [is] … broken, and the person senses that something is missing" (2012, p. 176). What is missing, for Lacan, is the father or any representative of a third party, crucial elements of the symbolic world that have never been present. Leader states:

A discontinuity occurs, breaching the co-coon they may have established until then with their lover, their friends, their baby or their work. They are suddenly forced to appeal to a symbolic element that isn't there. Without it, the feeling of perplexity may start ... (2012, p. 177)

The symbolic world then begins to unravel, like the wool in a knitted garment when a rent appears. A subsequent delusion is then a desperate attempt to repair the hole, to introduce a sense of order out of the perplexity.

Although Lacan's emphasis was upon the place of the father in the symbolic network, it may be that a shock removal or shift in any hitherto fixed coordinate in a person's inner identity, which delivers the sense of "I am not who I thought I was", can bring about a progressive disintegration of psychic structure. This can involve the sense of who one is in relation to a significant other person, such as the child's relationship with the mother, or indeed the father. Marked and sudden shifts in a mother's (or father's) demeanour, particularly when seemingly inexplicable, can have this effect of inducing perplexity and potential panic. The situation may be compounded when the child has no other person (such as the father) readily to turn to for comfort and help in understanding what is going on. Shock waves through the structure of the psyche and the symbolic network may occur whenever there is abuse or betrayal by a hitherto trusted or idealised figure, such as a teacher.

The unravelling of the symbolic world is a particular danger at certain stages of the adolescent process, when a loosening and reorganising of the earlier structures of meaning is an inherent feature. The afflicted adolescent may undergo periods of immense inarticulate anguish of feeling that nothing makes sense, nothing has any meaning, and nothing can be communicated.

The person with a narcissistic disorder may be struggling not only to maintain the pathological grandiose self and ward off the negative self-image, but also to defend above all against the ultimate catastrophe of having no self and complete disintegration of psychic structure and meaning.

CLINICAL ILLUSTRATION

Pam, a woman in her thirties, working as a legal executive, sought psychotherapeutic support from an analyst, Dr Forest, in relation to troubling experiences in her workplace. She also complained of abusive and thoughtless behaviour by members of her family, and also by various men with whom she had had brief relationships. Over time, it became apparent that not only did Pam lack a regular partner, she also appeared not to have any close friendships.

Initially, the therapeutic sessions appeared positive. Pam seemed to value the analyst's understanding and empathy. However, Dr Forest became increasingly uneasy, although he dismissed some early subtle feelings of foreboding. He noticed that so long as he maintained an empathic focus on Pam's experience of victimhood, along with an appreciation of her successes and positive qualities, she appeared soothed by the sessions. Interpretations of other people's motives were valued. However, if Dr Forest tried to explore the functions of Pam's own mind, she would become prickly and argumentative, complaining of feeling misunderstood and endeavouring to argue that the analyst was wrong. At times she would convey her view that Dr Forest was causing her great distress by his misunderstanding and making her condition worse. Dr Forest felt guilty and ashamed, and tried to make reparation by redoubling his efforts towards an empathic stance.

Sometimes, Pam's view of situations would seem somewhat paranoid, for example in her feelings that family members, or work colleagues, or even other organisations, were conspiring against her. When Dr Forest queried the reality of these, Pam argued that he was failing to perceive the awful truth of her situation. Dr Forest began to doubt his own perceptions and judgement – and, at times, even his sanity – particularly when Pam repeatedly accused him of being overly rigid and tied to his psychoanalytic theories.

Pam's life appeared full of distressing events where others had behaved in callous, wounding, or exploitative ways. If Dr Forest tried to explore Pam's own contribution to these, she would persuasively argue differently. He felt confined to a role of merely witnessing and mirroring Pam's perceptions.

Dr Forest's sense of being a rather incompetent analyst was intensified by Pam's success on occasion of persuading him to engage in actions outside the normal analytic frame, such as writing a letter of support when she was engaged in a legal dispute with her employer. Dr Forest was aware that such actions might be viewed by colleagues as inappropriate, but Pam had been so persistent with her demands and her persuasive arguments – for instance, that so much depended on the outcome of this dispute that petty analytic rules should surely be set aside on this occasion, and that Dr Forest was better placed than anyone to know the effect on her mental state of her firm's treatment of her, and that in fact there was no one else who could fulfil this function. Dr Forest wondered about discussing these issues in his peer supervision group but felt that his work with Pam had become so compromised and deviant that his feelings of shame inhibited him from doing so.

After several years of work, Dr Forest was uncomfortably and shamefully aware that Pam seemed not to be improving, yet she showed no sign of wanting to stop. He began to dread the prospect of being stuck with her indefinitely. The situation had worsened after Pam lost her job following the dispute with her employer and she had not been able to find further work. Her life circumstances had narrowed, living alone in rented accommodation, with a greatly reduced income. Dr Forest had felt obliged to reduce Pam's fee. He was aware of her dependence on him, as the only person she spoke to for much of each week. If he tried to introduce a consideration of when the therapy might end, Pam reacted with intense distress, conveying her sense of shock that he would even think of such a possibility when her life was so dire. Dr Forest's self-esteem progressively plummeted, and he was aware of feeling depressed, anxious, and to be sleeping badly.

Over the years there had been some exploration of Pam's early life and family circumstances. She was the youngest of three, with an older brother and sister. She reported feeling loved by her mother, with whom she felt she had a close relationship that she perceived as being envied by her siblings. Her father appeared more distant, an academic immersed in his historical research. There were occasional hints that her sense of being loved by her mother was somewhat conditional on her fitting her mother's image of how her daughter should think, feel, and behave – a kind of subtle unspoken snobbery on her mother's part. The impression was that Pam's mother would not express open disapproval or anger, but would simply become a little withdrawn, aloof, and less warm, when Pam deviated from the implicitly prescribed path of middle-class professional respectability. For example, when Pam had been a teenager and had bought a rather short skirt, similar to those of her peers, her mother had made no comment whatsoever, contrasting with her usual warm encouragement and compliments on Pam's appearance.

On one occasion, Dr Forest made an interpretation that seemed to move Pam deeply and began to lead to deeper and more constructive work. He had become aware of how closely, and often accurately, Pam monitored his moods and states of mind. Sometimes she would complain that he seemed "off" with her, that he appeared angry, or perhaps he was just inattentive, and that this was making her feel worse. She would demand that he return to his correct warm and empathic stance. Sometimes these demands would indeed make him angry and defensive, leading to an impasse, during which he would feel frankly wretched. During one such episode, Dr Forest suddenly blurted out that he thought Pam lived in dread of falling out of the realm of approval and of finding herself having no place anywhere in the world – that would be like existing in a state of not existing, and of being completely unknown. Pam looked shocked and was then tearful, saying softly that she had finally felt understood.

Gradually Pam and Dr Forest were able to explore the possibility of her life and state of being beyond the realm of her mother's prescribed image and place for her. She also began to recall further experiences of being painfully ignored by her mother, or, as she came to think of it, being "abolished" and "made extinct". This shift in perception was accompanied by moods of depression, and at times extreme anxiety – the kind that Kohut (1977) described as disintegration anxiety, occurring when the structures of the psyche begin to give way. Pam began slowly and painfully to appreciate that the patterns of hurt she experienced from others were modelled on her repudiated experiences of subtle rejection by her mother. In order to preserve the idealised images of her mother and of herself, she had needed to project these. The transference to Dr Forest had not been simply a historical repetition of her relationship with her mother, although it had contained this, but was also a distortion brought about by her need to protect her image of her mother. In the transference, Dr Forest had become at times the repudiated rejecting mother, as well as the distant and neglectful father. Much of the time, however, he was coerced into the function of preserving Pam's positive images of self and her mother – a role that did not quite correspond to the historical developmental transference, although in certain respects *she* was then in the role of her mother now exerting coercive control over Dr Forest. Pam's unconscious dread had been that if she did not maintain Dr Forest in his designated and restricted selfobject mirroring position, he might move into the place of her mother and she would once again be in the place of extinction.

In time, both Pam and Dr Forest began to feel better about themselves and each other.

COMMENTARY

Until the crucial shift into more constructive analytic exploration, Pam kept Dr Forest engaged
in the role of selfobject whose main function was
to soothe her with empathy and mirroring of her
positive images of self and her mother. To this end,
any feelings or experiences that were at odds with
these images had to be repudiated and projected. They found expression in Pam's many dramas
of upset with people in her current life, including occasionally Dr Forest. She had to monitor
Dr Forest's moods and states of mind in order to
guard against the danger that he would become
the warded off annihilating mother. Pam's ultimate
dread was more than losing the positive image
of herself (and her mother) – it was of having *no*
image, of having no place. It is this fate of being
unknown and unseen, of having no psychic and
symbolic coordinates, that may be feared at the
most profound level.

Pam subjected Dr Forest to subtle forms of coercive control, rewarding him for compliant empathic mirroring and punishing him for expressing more autonomy of thought and perception. In this way, she identified with the repudiated aspects of her mother. Dr Forest was manoeuvred into the place of the inadequate shame-laden one, while Pam could remain in the position of the righteous victim. At times, when at his most disoriented, Dr Forest was in danger of entering into the dreaded place of no place.

It was when Dr Forest was inspired to find a way of articulating this presymbolic dread (Mollon, 2001a), a terror that seems beyond words, that Pam felt enabled to confront the flawed foundations of her psychic structure.

In this example, as in many others, we see that pathological narcissism functions in part as a defence against unbearable aspects of the human condition – our physical and emotional vulnerability, and the potential for disintegration anxiety. In our pathological narcissism, we seek to force the world to act in accord with our will.

3

The imaginary self

Much of what we think of as narcissism is really a preoccupation with image. The self that is inflated, or denigrated, or defended at all costs, is imaginary – a fantasy!

When operating within the "reality position", a person will be engaged in one or more of the related activities of:

- Performing work as a means of "earning a living" – expending energy in return for monetary reward. Work will often involve problem solving – such as fixing a car or a broken fence, solving a scientific puzzle, managing a business, or supporting a family financially

- Seeking to develop, repair, or maintain an attachment relationship
- Engaging in artistic or other cultural pursuits, or sports
- Resting.

None of these is inherently narcissistic. All may result in healthy satisfaction and pleasure, and all except resting depend on some degree of relatedness to others and the shared social order.

By contrast, narcissistic activities are concerned with the preservation or nurturance of the imaginary self. This can intrude into and distort activities that are essentially non-narcissistic. For example, whether in the context of work or an attachment relationship, a narcissistic person may become preoccupied with preserving a particular self-image, or of coercing others to support this image. In a workplace, this can be to the detriment of focusing on the realities of the task and ensuring it is accomplished in an efficient and effective manner.

Current societal trends encourage narcissism, insofar as there is an excessive focus on image and appearance, including the image of the body. These sociocultural factors combine with personal dynamics. A state of body dysmorphia is inherently narcissistic, involving a preoccupation with the image and appearance of the body, albeit an image with a negative valence. There is a wound behind the body-focused narcissism – a state of feeling unloved and unlovable, displaced and condensed to a body part. During certain states of mind, such as when embarking upon an extramarital affair, a woman would become obsessed with the thought that she would be more desirable and loved if her lips and buttocks were bigger. These states of mind were characterised by her desire to be desired, and her pleasure in flirtation. Her concern for the men she attracted was minimal, and thus at these times her engagement with others was of a narcissistic rather than lovingly relating nature. By contrast, when she emerged from these states of mind, she felt somewhat horrified at what she viewed in retrospect as her highly self-absorbed condition. In her case (as in that of many others), the original wound was a combination of feeling ignored by her narcissistic mother and failing to evoke a compensatory and validating love from her father. Her mother's narcissism was reflected in a preoccupation with clothes, jewellery, and glamour – and thus the narcissistic wound was transmitted to her daughter who then sought her own narcissistic solutions in plans for bodily augmentation surgery.

TRAPPED IN THE MOTHER'S REPUDIATED (IMAGINARY) SELF

The following situation seems to be very common, perhaps more so among women. In this developmental scenario, the narcissistic mother is highly invested in her imaginary self-image – as glamorous, beautiful, desirable, devoted mother, selfless giver, morally superior being, etc. Aspects of reality that are incongruent with this idealised self-image are projected onto her child, who is then unconsciously treated as her own bad self. For example, one woman, Sally, was repeatedly criticised by her mother who would tell her she was a failure and a disappointment in every way. Sally's career, choice of husband, and behaviour towards her mother were all deemed reprehensible in various respects. She could never please this mother. As we explored these matters, Sally remarked that perhaps her mother had always resented her because her existence was a sign and a reminder of her mother's extramarital affair. This seemed almost certainly correct, but the further point that helped Sally understand her developmental predicament was that her mother had a narcissistic disturbance whereby she could not tolerate a reality that challenged her idealised self-image as the perfect mother. Instead of acknowledging her own sense of failure and regret, Sally's mother projected these qualities into her daughter, who was then treated as embodying her own disavowed defective self. As an illustration of her mother's narcissistic nature, Sally described not only her preoccupation with clothes and appearance, but also recalled a disturbing incident. When Sally was a young girl, she had come home from school and found her stepfather slumped in a chair. She had called a neighbour, who confirmed the impression the stepfather had died. Since this was a time before telephones of any kind were readily available, Sally had then run into town to the shop where her mother worked. She blurted out to her mother the sad and shocking news, to which her mother's immediate response was, "How dare you come into the shop wearing slippers!" Thus, in the face of profoundly important and potentially deeply painful information, Sally's mother's preoccupation with image and appearance took precedence. No doubt this can be understood in part as a rapid defensive response against potential depressive pain, but this is indeed the nature of the narcissistic defence of the imaginary self.

Often the narcissistic mother's disapproval

is directed against her child's natural desire for independence and a degree of autonomy. There may be a loving closeness when the child is very young, but this is withdrawn as the child attempts to initiate or explore any autonomy of movement, thought, or desire. In such a situation, as Masterson (Masterson & Rinsley, 1980) states, the child can either feel "good but fused with mother" or "separate and bad". The child feels that any step towards independence of direction, thought, perception, or desire is a developmental crime. As an adult, such a person may indeed achieve independence and separation from the narcissistic mother, but at the cost of a persisting and pervasive sense of guilt that may lead to self-sabotage in a variety of ways.

This is a situation depicted in horrifying starkness by Kohut (1979) in his paper "The Two Analyses of Mr Z", now commonly regarded as autobiographical (Strozier, 2001). At a point in the second analysis, informed by Kohut's emerging theory of self-psychology, when Mr Z is beginning to achieve an inner separation-individuation from his mother, he has a dream consisting simply of his mother with her back to him. This was accompanied by the most intense anxiety he had ever experienced (disintegration anxiety). Kohut's explanation was that this image not only represented his mother's turning her psychological back on her son whenever he attempted a forward developmental step of individuation, but, even more deeply, expressed the fear that she had no face – that if he became a separate self, there would be no mirroring empathic mother, that he would be psychologically completely alone.

A recurrent theme in all Kohut's published clinical illustrations is the absence, or relative emotional absence, of the father. In most of these examples, the child has been trapped in an unsatisfactory dyad with the mother, with insufficient contact with, or support from, the father as a third party to help facilitate the separation from the mother (Mollon, 1993).

The strength of a child's desire to please a parent and thereby feel loved can trump all other motives. Sometimes it is the love of a father that is (unsuccessfully) sought, partly because the father is seen as a key to the escape from the potential trap of the dyad with the mother. One man had the thought, after his father died, "Well I might as well die now – there's nothing left to live for." This led him to reflect on how his whole life, up until that point, had been unconsciously structured around attempts to win his father's approval. To this end, he had many impressive career and social achievements, none of which brought him satisfaction or his father's admiration. At various points in his life, he perceived his employers as demanding, unappreciative, and uncaring, all clearly transference-based perceptions and associated with rage and the pain of feeling uncared for.

THE MIMETIC SELF

Despite an illusory substantiality, the human sense of self is flimsy and fragile, a mirage prone to dissolution when its structure is examined. Lacan

(1937) noted that the earliest sense of self is a false image – the infant is captured by a mirror. For quite a long period, human societies have made prominent use of mirrors – shiny surfaces that reflect an image. The literal mirror forms a template for the capture of the self by social mirrors, including the current ubiquitous social media.

The mirror-based images of self are facilitated also by mirror neurons, which generate within the emotional states perceived in the other. A child may cry when it sees another child fall over. Some appear to have more of a mirror neuronal response than others. A man diagnosed with Asperger's told me he could never tell what another person was feeling, and that if he saw someone crying his true response was to find this amusing, although he was not inherently unkind or sadistic. By contrast, a young woman described to me how she was constantly in a state of anxiety, fearing she might lose herself because if she looked at another person, she might become that person. She noticed that if she looked, she would somehow feel that person's emotions and mental state (similar experiences are described by Williams, 1998). She felt obliged to engage in internal obsessional rituals in order to ward off this merger of identities.

From the beginning of our lives, we are continually, but unconsciously, imitating, miming, and identifying with others – with their bodily movements, posture, speech, facial expressions, attitudes, modes of emotional expression. Bruce Wilshire, an actor and phenomenological philosopher, wrote of the fundamentally mimetic nature of human identity:

> *Human individuals are beings of weak and precarious identity. Each is a vulnerable and absolutely particular body, yet each must define itself according to general ideas and communal patterns. (1982, p. 294)*

Writing well before the emergence of social media and its malign captivation of our culture, he observed:

We seem to be as primitively engulfed in our everyday companions and in their opinions of us, and in modish thinkers, party chiefs, rock stars, models of taste, consumption, or aggression – and in the masses that follow them – as ever the human race was engulfed in anything. Professors and scholars are no exception. (1982, p. 293)

If we observe a flock of birds in flight, we may be struck by the astonishing way in which the entire group seems to keep in synch, each bird changing direction at the same time, and we may ponder how such coordination and communication of intention comes about. As human beings, we like to view ourselves as at least somewhat independent in our thinking and choices. Wilshire's observations suggest we are also very much herd animals, prone to group behaviour and group thinking. Fashions occur not only in clothing but in all manner of behaviours and attitudes. Psychoanalysts are far from immune to fashions of thought. Around the world, different groups of psychoanalysts have developed their own styles and nuances of both theory and technique – and yet representatives of each group will earnestly debate and advocate for their particular perspective, as if the habits of their own analytic neighbourhood express a privileged truth.

THE EVOLVING SELF-IMAGE

A self-image is necessary for functioning in the social world – part of the internal map of social relationships. In infancy and childhood, these images can be fantastical and either grandiose or intensely denigrated. It is quite normal for a young child to imagine having all manner of magic powers, or being a figure of high status in a secret world. In the course of normal development, these images become more realistic, and more clearly differentiated.

One of the great theorists of the period of psychoanalytic ego psychology in the US, Edith Jacobson (1971), provided some vivid examples of patients whose representations of self had either failed to develop optimally or had undergone a regression to unrealistic or undifferentiated states. She described a twenty-seven-year-old woman, Mrs P, who developed a schizophrenic state when her second marriage was breaking down. It was her second episode. Prior to her illness, she had been ambitious and "predominantly megalomanic, supercilious, cold, and brittle" and "forever in search of her own identity" and believed she was a genius (p. 253) – a view of herself that she shared with her schizophrenic mother. Jacobson writes that when Mrs P was confronted by the realities of her limitations, she would respond with increased grandiosity and a refusal to accept the facts of the situation until failure was inevitable, at which point she would become depressed.

In an agitated state, Mrs P had contacted Dr Jacobson, saying she was worried about her husband Larry, whom she feared would commit suicide because she was planning to leave him. By contrast, she declared herself to be feeling on top of the world because she did not need her husband anymore. Following this interview, she went home and flew into a rage with Larry, but then calmly packed some belongings and left for a hotel, where she then developed a severe state of excitement, singing loudly and making lots of noise. When Dr Jacobson was called to her, Mrs P pulled her to the couch where she was sitting, saying:

> *Let us be close. I have made a great philosophical discovery. Do you know the difference between closeness, likeness, sameness, and oneness? Close is close, as with you; when you are like somebody, you are only* like *the other, you and he are two; sameness – you are the same as the other, but he is still he and you are you; but oneness is not two – it is one, that's horrible – Horrible! (p. 253)*

She then leapt up from the couch in panic, pushing Dr Jacobson away, saying she did not want to be too close because she did not want to be Dr Jacobson. She then became elated, declaring repeatedly that she was a genius, before going on to state that she had died and that her soul had gone and she was nothing.

At the hospital, Mrs P became depressed. After some months, she took on the role of an "attendant aide", conspicuously imitating the gestures and behaviour of the psychiatrist.

Over a long period of time, Mrs P's relationships displayed a pattern of imitation, followed by triumphant elation and declaration of not needing the other, culminating in depression. Her accompanying self-images easily fused with images of the other, and were of a grandiose and magical nature, alternating with contrasting images of a depleted and dead self.

In this example, Jacobson did not provide much information about the origins of Mrs P's disturbance. However, in an earlier book (Jacobson, 1965) she gave a very clear example of the thwarted evolution of the self-image in the case of a young man who suffered his first psychotic paranoid breakdown at the age of fifteen. Jacobson observed and treated the boy between his eighteenth and twenty-third year, a period during which he was unable to relate to peers and veered between paranoid rages at his parents and extreme submission to them. He believed that all wives tried to kill their husbands. His sexual fantasies were sadomasochistic, in which he would identify either as a sadistic dictator or his victim. He would experience urges to rape or strangle girls he saw in the street, or else castrate himself, although outwardly he was extremely polite. His sense of self and identity were extremely disturbed, and he would complain that he did not know who he was, and had no goals, beliefs, or ideals, and no consistency or coherence in his experience of self.

Jacobson described the boy's parents as "uniquely narcissistic", dutiful but unloving and "completely unaware of their child's needs" (1965, p. 215). They told Jacobson that when they caught him masturbating at the age of nine, they wept and told him he would become insane. From this time onwards, they had constantly watched him, accompanying him to the toilet, and his mother would rub ointment on his "sore penis" every night – a practice that caused erections and obsessional masturbation with incestuous fantasies. The mother had not allowed the boy to play with other children, but after another mother described her as overprotective, she sent him alone on a long journey to New York, during which he got lost and became terrified. Jacobson described how the parents appeared very satisfied that from an early age, he had been "precisely the way we wanted him to be, precisely the way we are ourselves" (p. 216).

In Jacobson's view, the boy's instability and fragility of his identity and ego reflected his struggles with intense rage provoked by the smothering of his autonomy and natural developmental processes. He remembered fantasies from as early as seven, in which he was strapped to his mother's breast, flying straight to hell. He remarked, "I hated her so much that I wanted her to go to hell, but being chained to her, I had to go to hell with her" (p. 216). His psychotic breakdown expressed his frantic efforts to throw off his enslavement and inhibitions "by sending the overpowerful super-ego-ego mother to hell". She adds: "The result was chaos, and his breakdown did drive his mother to despair" (p. 216). Rather starkly, this was the final sentence of Jacobson's book.

THE IMPOSED IMAGE OF OWNERSHIP

Some forms of narcissism are so horrifying that they can appropriately attract descriptions such as "toxic", "malignant", and criminal. Sometimes overt, and sometimes hidden, the encounter with these states is always profoundly shocking – an experience of being suddenly face to face with an utterly cold, psychopathic sense of entitlement, a delusional belief in one person's inherent superiority over another. The person possessed of malignant narcissism may appear superficially charming, perhaps even loving – but this is a cover for a ruthless assertion of the unlimited rights of the pathological grandiose self. These qualities may be disguised as love.

For example, an attractive woman was pursued over a period of some months by a seemingly loving man whose position in the world signified high status and wealth. Although she liked this man, she felt there was no basis for a long-term relationship and so she attempted to end their involvement. The man first tried to persuade her against this, with flattery, expressions of affection, gifts, and promises of all the material and social benefits he could offer her. When his entreaties failed, he became threatening. He declared that no other man would ever have her – that he would arrange a murder of any man she had a relationship with, and that he would also harm members of her family. He said he would always know what she was doing. Revealing his hidden pathological grandiose self, he declared that she had no right to end their relationship when she had become so important to him and he had decided she would be his wife. The woman was utterly shaken by the confrontation with the man's delusional belief that since he wanted her, this desire took complete precedence over her own feelings. His apparent love was clearly not remotely loving but was instead a disguised expression of profound hatred for the woman's autonomy and existence as a separate being with her own desires, goals, and preferences. His grandiose self could not tolerate her independence of desire and her capacity to say no. Her declining of his plans for her collided with his hidden delusion of entitlement and ownership. Until this point, he had been able to "pass" as a refined, cultured, and loving man.

Malignant narcissism of this kind can also be found among certain child sexual abusers, who attain positions of power in organisations or institutions where they can fulfil their desires with little restraint. Such individuals may again appear superficially charming, particularly when engaged in grooming their victim – but the charm is a form of cynical control. It may later be combined with naked threats of violence and invalidation. Far from expressing any love, such paedo*philia* is a form of hatred, and can involve a sadistic pleasure in destroying a child's soul, distorting their personality development, and imprinting a psychic tattoo, an invisible branding of ownership on his or her future sexuality.

The person with toxic and malignant narcissism is unlikely to seek psychotherapeutic help – but if he or she does, the therapist will be subject to subtle threats, seductions, and forms of coercive control. Normal professional boundaries may be crossed, one small step at a time, until the relationship is profoundly compromised. The narcissistic client will exploit the therapist's shame and fears of exposure in the service of further control.

Narcissism hates love – because love requires recognising and accepting the other's separateness, autonomy, and ultimate unknowability.

FEATURES AND WARNING SIGNS OF COERCIVE AND CONTROLLING RELATIONSHIPS

The narcissistic agent who engages in coercive and controlling behaviour may not initially appear narcissistic (Walmsley-Johnson, 2018). Perpetrators of narcissistic abuse are commonly, but not exclusively, men and may be perceived as charming, amusing, and devoted (Bancroft. 2002; Stark, 2007). Such a man may go to great lengths to appear thoughtful and caring, as if his sole object in life is to please his beloved, overwhelming her or him with gifts and innumerable gestures of love and kindness. However, these displays of love and intense attention may alternate unpredictably with periods of cold withdrawal or disappearance – strategies that are sometimes advocated in some popular guides to seduction. The result is that the partner then feels confused and disoriented – and craving the love "high" that she or he has become addicted to.

This repeating pattern of love-bombing followed by withdrawal may begin to combine with subtle put-downs and criticisms that have the effect of undermining confidence and self-esteem (Lynch, 2013). It is a gradual process.

Another crucial component is the wearing away of the victim's trust in her or his perception of reality. The malignant narcissist will state that certain events the victim remembers did not happen or happened in quite a different way. This continual rewriting of history has an active distorting quality that goes beyond the normal phenomenon whereby each person perceives an event from his or her own perspective and inner models of reality. History is rewritten to support the narcissist's self-image and the positive image he presents to his victim. Gradually, the victim increasingly doubts her or his own perception. It is a process sometimes referred to as "gaslighting" – an allusion to a 1938 play in which a husband manipulates the brightness of the gas lights and other features of the environment but tells his wife she is imagining these events.

The malignant narcissist will complain that his

beloved does not love him, and may accuse them of infidelity – an accusation that may reflect his own activities. He may display emotional pain, in such a way that is convincing to his victim partner, who may try ever harder to show love and devotion.

Active discouraging of the victim's contact with friends and wider family is another key feature. The function of this is to prevent the person having access to alternative perspectives that might question the version of reality presented by the abuser. This strategy also increases the victim's dependence on the abuser. Sometimes the victim is discouraged from working, increasing their financial dependence.

As the victim's mental health deteriorates in response to this systematic psychological corrosion, the perpetrator presents himself as her saviour – the only one she can rely on. Seeking help from a doctor or counsellor-psychotherapist is discouraged.

In some cases, these toxic relational patterns progress to violence. The perpetrator protests, "Look what you made me do!" This increases the victim's sense of shame. Any thought of leaving is countered by the perpetrator's assertion that no one else would want such a worthless and incompetent person – a claim that finds fertile ground in the victim's now shattered self-esteem.

Recovery from the effects of coercive and controlling relational trauma can be a slow and difficult process, working against the victim's intensely layered shame and self-blame and identification with the aggressor (Bogat, Garcia, & Levendosky, 2013).

The perpetrator's own mental equilibrium may be fragile, using the other as a vessel for projected feelings of weakness and vulnerability. He or she will have an unconscious awareness of the malign narcissistic game they are engaged in, creating intensifying potential shame, which must in turn be projected into the victim – thus, creating an ever-greater addiction to the narcissistic abuse. When deprived of the victim, he or she may decompensate, becoming more overtly disturbed, or may seek another replacement victim.

IS THERE ANYTHING BEHIND THE IMAGE?

The psychodynamics of narcissism concern the manipulation and preservation of the image of the self. But is there anything behind the image? Is there a self beyond an image and a network of signifiers? The Lacanian position would suggest no. Nobus (2000) writes:

> *In Lacan's view ... the degree to which human beings are convinced that they possess a strong identity is more indicative of psychosis than anything else ... behind all these identifications there is no essential core, no anchored true identity. The me does not operate as part of a larger "self", nor does it shield a hidden self. It is but a surface or wall behind which there is nothing to be found. (pp. 196–197)*

We might indeed say that identity is an illusion, albeit one that is fiercely defended, that *all human selves are false selves*, based on identifications with the images and roles available within the particular culture into which the child is born. However, I believe there is more – that there is a deep source of being that exists beyond the illusion and the symbolic order (Faber, 2013). The "true self" is always an unknown evolving self (Groddeck, 1929). Part of our task as psychotherapists is to facilitate the connection to this unknown.

THE 'TOTALITARIAN EGO' AND THE LEFT HEMISPHERE.

In its capacity as an agent of illusion, the ego is "totalitarian" (Greenwald, 1980). It seeks to dominate and control perceptions of self and other, and to foreclose or limit awareness of the ineffable, the realm which Bion (1965) termed "O". The ego wants to say that the ego's world is all there is (Schucman, 1975). From a neuroscience perspective, this reflects the linear logic of the linguistic left hemisphere of the brain, categorising and judging, usurping and denying the holistic vision and illu-mination of the right hemisphere (McGilchrist, 2009; Tweedy, 2013). All of narcissistic pathology stems from this left brain tyranny and its fear of the unknown evolving self of the right brain. To the extent we can counter this, we set our patients (and ourselves) free.

4

Narcissism and sexual trauma

Narcissistic injuries are wounds to our self-esteem, resulting from humiliations, slights, shaming, feeling misunderstood, being treated without empathy or respect for individuality (Mollon, 1984, 1986, 1993). Some such wounds attack aspects of our core sense of identity and self-worth.

Narcissistic injuries are saturated with the emotion of shame. When we feel loved, accepted, and understood, the emotional tone of the experience is one of freedom and expansion. At such moments we may reach out uninhibitedly to connect with others and express warmth and affection. The primordial version of this is the baby at the breast, basking in the warmth of the mother's smile and loving eyes. By contrast, if the mother is not smiling, or is detached, uninvolved, showing a blank face, or openly rejecting, the baby will retreat and display early indicators of shame (Tronick, Als, Adamson, Wise, & Brazelton, 1978). When we experience rejection or an absence of acceptance, we feel shame. Our life energy does not flow outwards expansively, but instead retreats into reverse. This is the essence of shame, which is the core affect of narcissistic injury (Mollon, 1984, 1986, 1993, 2002).

One of the odd features of human sexuality is that it gathers around the deepest wounds to the self and creates a kind of healing by making these the focus of sexual excitement. Robert Stoller described this process in a series of books on sexuality (e.g., Stoller, 1976). Kohut observed similar developments, so much so that he referred to compulsive sexual fantasies as "sexualised statements about narcissistic injury" (1971, p. 71).

Kohut (1971) described Mr A, whose homosexual fantasies usually involved a theme of enslaving a strong and virile man whom he would masturbate and thereby drain of his power. According to Kohut's understanding, these expressed in a sexualised form Mr A's longing for an infusion of strength and perfection from an idealised man, originally the father. What was missing was part of the inner structure of the self – the idealised values, and the potential self-esteem that comes from living up to these. In place of this inner structure, Mr A had substituted a sexualised sense of triumph in stealing qualities of power and strength from an external ideal. Kohut saw such "sexualised statements about narcissistic injury" as analogous to the theoretical formulations of the analyst, both of which are ways of representing the patient's core narcissistic injuries and tensions – with the difference that the sexual fantasies are in opposition to insight and are created in the service of pleasure and relief from narcissistic tensions (which are not essentially sexual tensions, despite the surface appearance).

In another example, Mr E would often engage in dangerous voyeuristic pursuits, particularly gazing at other men's genitals in public toilets, during separations from the analyst or when feeling misunderstood by the analyst. In the course of the analytic work, Mr E recalled the first episode of voyeurism as a young child. It took place at a country fair, when he had asked his mother to admire his skill when flying high on a swing. His mother, ill and depressed, showed little interest and the little Mr E felt deflated, humiliated, and drained of joy. He turned away from her and visited the toilet. Then, "Driven by a force which he understood only now, but for which he could now, also, recall the appropriate feeling tone, he looked at a man's genital and, merging into it, felt at one with the power and strength that it symbolised" (1971, p. 159).

Regarding analytic technique with sexual fantasies and activities, Kohut advised that on the whole it is best not to focus on them or attempt to interpret their details. As he put it, "[S]uch fantasies are not made for insight; they are made for enjoyment" (1996, p. 9). Since he found that focusing on the sexual fantasy can encourage the wish for sexual gratification, he would, instead, pose the question of why the fantasy had emerged at that particular point. He would endeavour to reveal how the fantasy related to the transference in terms of what development-supporting responses the patient was seeking from the analyst and how the analyst was experienced as failing to provide these. Thus, the patient would be helped to understand the non-sexual meaning of the transference desires and of what therefore was developmentally missing.

During the later analytic work, Mr E was able to reduce his compulsion to resort to crudely sexualised solutions to the dangers to his fragile self-structure when the selfobject analyst was missing. One weekend he arrived at an artistic alternative. He painted a picture of the analyst, but with the eyes and nose replaced by an image of the analysand. This vividly expressed the mirroring role of the selfobject. When Mr E looked at the analyst, he saw himself held in mind and reflected empathically. The image of the analyst and that of the analysand were held within the same structure – and were thus a visual expression of the fused word "selfobject" (Kohut, 1971, pp. 130–132).

Some sexual fantasies express what was missing – such as responsiveness from Mr E's mother – whilst others express narcissistic injuries based on what was too much *present*. An example of the latter is Kohut's case of Mr Z (1979), whose mother was pathologically controlling and intrusive, continually inspecting his body, including his penis. Mr Z developed masochistic sexual fantasies of being controlled by powerful women and used as a human toilet. All such sexual fantasies are driven by a weakened or disintegrating self. A formula for understanding unusual sexual fantasies is: (1) remove the sexual element and see what kind of relational activity is represented; (2) consider whether the fantasy represents something that happened in the child's early life, or something that was needed but did not happen; (3) explore what triggers the fantasy, and what is the current trigger – the latter may be a narcissistic injury (feeling ignored, misunderstood, disregarded, shamed, or humiliated) by a significant person, including the psychotherapist.

A consistent feature of Kohut's clinical work was his focus on what was experienced as *missing* in the relationship with the analyst, and on the patient's response to this absence. His clinical discoveries and theories were analogous to a photographic negative of psychopathology – what was *present* being an indicator of what was *absent* in the patient's early environment and psychic structure (Mollon, 2001a). This novel and subtle perspective may have contributed to a widespread misunderstanding of his approach. For example, many have assumed that Kohut advocated active "mirroring" or even praise and admiration, or other narcissistic gratifications. Here is what he said in his lectures at the Chicago Institute:

You don't have to mirror the patient to be effective as his analyst. That really is a total mistake. The meaning of mirroring, the essence of that concept, is not that you have to play act with your patient and praise him and respond to him and say that he is wonderful. No such nonsense. But you do have to show the patient over and over again how he defensively retreats because he expects that he will not get what he wants and that he doesn't dare to let himself know what he wants … *Any patient who gets an unrealistic overdose of praise, who gets more than just an honestly empathic understanding of what his aspirations are, will be affronted. He will very soon be very angry at you. (Kohut, 1996, p. 373, emphasis added)*

Kohut postulated that patients who sexualise narcissistic tensions may do so partly because of a deficiency in the neutralising functions of the psyche. The concept of neutralisation is relatively unfamiliar to modern psychoanalytic practitioners, particularly in Britain, but it was an important theoretical construct within the work of Hartmann (e.g., 1964) and colleagues, denoting the transformation of raw instinctual (sexual and aggressive) energy into a more "neutral" form, suitable for use by the higher psychic functions. Kohut theorised that the capacity to neutralise sexual and aggressive impulses derives in part from the selfobject functions provided by the caregivers and teachers in the child's early life. These form important ego functions, allowing the child and later the adult to function in the world of culture and civilisation. Kohut observed that some patients represented these de-aggressifying and desexualising functions by dreams of books and libraries. Such symbols represent the secondary, as opposed to primary process, of reality-based, culturally recognised, and socially approved activities – and Lacan's realm of the symbolic order.

Kohut gave the example (1971, p. 173) of a patient who represented mounting sexual tension during sleep by a dream of riding on a fast-moving train; on getting up and walking from carriage to carriage, he realised he had left his books on his seat and went back to collect them, only to find, to his horror, that his carriage had become disconnected from the part of the train on which he was now riding. Kohut viewed this dream as expressing his alarmed realisation that his ego had been hijacked by sexual excitement and had lost access to the drive-regulating and drive-elaborating functions of the secondary process. The patient suffered from premature ejaculation, a condition that may express a deficiency in the capacity to contain and regulate sexual arousal and channel it in the service of mutually pleasurable lovemaking.

THE DEPLETED SELF, HIDDEN BEHIND THE OEDIPAL CONFLICT

Much of conventional psychoanalysis is concerned with intense emotional passions and conflicts of childhood – such as the oedipal child's hatred of parental coupling and feelings of exclusion, rivalry, and hatred, or situations of emotional and sexual overstimulation or abuse. While Kohut recognised that such circumstances present challenges to the child's development, he also emphasised the difficulties that can arise where the home atmosphere is characterised by an absence of parental liveliness and sexuality:

> *The child wants to intrude into the bedroom of the parents. The doors are closed. He feels deeply rejected. That is all true. That is the tragedy of healthy pathology, and we must deal with it when it has pathological consequences. But to grow up in a family in which there are no closed doors, and no sex behind doors, a family in which there are old grandparents walking around, thinking about how many more years they have left to live – that is really a different atmosphere. … It is in these families that*

*children say, "What kind of world is this?
Here I am proudly exhibiting myself, and
there is only silence." (1996, pp. 265–266)*

Kohut considered that in such environments, a child's oedipal conflicts, passions, and rivalries may be intentionally (but non-consciously) intensified in order to provide stimulation for the depleted self. This observation is similar to phenomena readily observed with certain children and adults with ADHD, in which the stimulation-seeking brain will stir up interpersonal conflicts and drama in order to counter the dreaded states of boredom of the depleted self (Mollon, 2015).

EFFECTS OF CHILDHOOD ABUSE TRAUMA ON THE DEVELOPING SELF

Normal development takes place through the availability of the responsive selfobject aspects of the caregivers. Via a combination of good enough empathic responsiveness and optimum failure of empathy, the child survives the non-traumatic failures of the selfobject so that a process of "transmuting internalisation" takes place. Through this process, the child internalises gradually the functions once performed by the selfobject. The result is an increasing capacity to regulate emotions, impulses, and arousal, to mentalise, and to achieve empathy and compassion for the self.

Abuse by a caregiver acts as a profound reversal of the normal development-enhancing functions of the selfobject. Instead of promoting maturation towards adulthood and independence, this reversed selfobject functions to prevent maturation of narcissism and the establishment of a coherent sense of self, and the child may be propelled backwards to the position of the fragmented self. Under good enough circumstances, the child turns to the selfobject when hurt, whether this be emotional or physical. When the selfobject itself is the source of the trauma, this cannot happen unless the child's perceptions are dissociated (Mollon, 1996, 2001b).

For example, a patient with a dissociative identity disorder (DID) had some personalities that reported her stepfather had sexually abused her over a number of years, whilst other personalities spoke of all the ways he made her feel special and loved. Rather than a self making use of repression to avoid awareness of a distressing experience (a horizontal split), this is an alteration in the self as a central and coherent organisation of experience (a vertical split). It is not an alteration in the *content* of consciousness but a change in the very *structure* of consciousness and the self. As a result of compartmentalisation and forcible unintegration of contradictory experiences, multiple and mutually incongruent representations of both self and other may occur. Under these conditions, there may be no central self, no sense of "I" that persists through varying and conflicting experiences and has continuity across time. Instead, there may be a group of disparate personalities, each of whom may at any particular moment regard him/herself as *the* self.

Reactions of numbing and detachment are

common responses to trauma, even in the absence of the severe structural dissociations of DID, and these may result in the child's experience of self and of the surrounding world feeling unfamiliar. If such reactions become chronic, then the child's sense of connection to self and other will be dislocated, giving rise to unrooted particles of consciousness that do not cohere in the normal way. There may be a pervasive backdrop of anxiety, against which there is a limited sense of continuity of self. These may be described as "mutilated states of consciousness" (Mollon, 1998). Instead of a sense of being supported and held securely, as connoted by Grotstein's (1981) concept of the "background selfobject of primary identification", there may be a state of continual dread of falling apart and disintegrating: the very fabric on which the tapestry of self-experience is to be woven is so flimsy it is full of tears and holes. There may be no firm foundations to the personality, such that the metaphor of a structural fault (Balint, 1968) is very apt.

Milder instances of sexual molestation by a previously admired or idealised figure, such as a teacher, doctor, or family friend, may still give rise to profound disillusionment shock – and a sense of pervasive distrust in the adult world. The child's previously outgoing emotions and energy may shift subtly into reverse.

SEVEN DIMENSIONS OF THE EXPERIENCE OF SELF – ALL DAMAGED BY CHILDHOOD SEXUAL ABUSE

In *The Fragile Self* (Mollon, 1993), I described a taxonomy of seven dimensions of potential disturbance in the experience of self, all of which are damaged by childhood sexual abuse (Mollon, 2001a). These were:

- The differentiation of self and other
- The subjective self – the sense of agency
- The objective self – self-esteem and self-image
- Structure and organisation – the sense of coherence, cohesion, and integrity of the self

- The balance between subjective and objective self (the extent of excessive accommodation to the other vs excessive disregard of the other)
- Illusions of self-sufficiency
- The sense of lineage – the sense of connection to origins, a parental and cultural line.

A child who has been extensively abused and mind-controlled will inhabit the version of reality imposed by the abuser – and this may include the illusion that the abuser will always have control over the victim. As a result, the *differentiation* of self and other will be impaired, as well as the *sense of agency*. In the realm of the *objective self*, the child's (and later the adult's) self-esteem and self-image will be negative in the extreme, believing he or she must have been very bad for the abuse to have occurred. Because of the incomplete separation of self and other, the child cannot hate the abuser without hating the self.

The abused child (or adult in a relationship

of coercive control) will identify with the image forced upon him or her by the abuser – a process of imposed identity. Such an image may include qualities of being bad, helpless, worthless, unlovable, etc. The abuser behaves in such a way as to force the victim to experience the self in terms of that highly negative image.

The development of a *coherent self* depends upon a secure and stable selfobject background, wherein the child's feelings, needs, and autonomy are recognised and supported. By contrast, the child who is extensively abused may develop what is effectively a shattered self, a chaotic plethora of self-images, lacking coherence and integration. This is most apparent in those who develop the extreme condition of DID, a structure of self in which there are multiple personality states, each with their own attitude, identity, mode of cognition, and memories (Mollon, 1996, 2001b).

The *balance between subjective and objective self* is inevitably skewed towards accommodation to the other when a child has been repeatedly abused by a caregiver, since it is the latter's will, desire, and agenda that prevail. Instead of being supported by the selfobject functions of empathy and other development-enhancing responses, performing as a debased selfobject for the other will become the life-role of the abused child. The natural order of the adults providing care for the child is reversed and perverted, so that the child's role is to satisfy the needs and desires of the adult.

The abused child's *sense of lineage* will be permeated with shame and self-loathing, especially if the perpetrator is a parent. Shame for the victim self, and shame at being the child of an abuser, combine to create a toxic tidal wave of self-hatred and self-directed rage. Such intense shame is itself a trauma, flooding the ego and sweeping away all vestiges of self-esteem. In such states, all empathy for the self is lost.

Because the abused child has not experienced protection and secure, trusting attachment, he or she will not easily be able later to form relationships of trust and healthy dependence. For many such people, seeking intimacy, dependence, and trust will be perceived unconsciously, or even consciously, as profoundly dangerous (Mollon, 1996). Instead, the person may pursue *illusions of self-sufficiency*, taking flight or unconsciously sabotaging relationships whenever attachment or trust becomes a potential possibility. In the context of psychotherapy, it is a commonplace that the more the client feels trust towards the therapist, the greater the unconsciously perceived danger, since to trust is felt to be utter folly.

In the context of an absence of a reliable caregiving early environment, some people who suffer childhood abuse develop rigid and oppressive internal organisations analogous to oppressive political systems or mafia gangs (Rosenfeld, 1971). Sometimes, but not always, expressed as internal voices, these controlling parts of the psyche can become very active under certain conditions deemed as forbidden – such as if the person reveals secrets of the abuse or if he or she moves towards trusting the therapist.

5

The roots and structure of narcissistic disturbance

FOUR METHODS FOR CREATING NARCISSISTIC DISTURBANCE

Much of the preceding discussion can be summed up in the following four schematic scenarios. These all involve a failure to nurture the development of the child's infantile narcissistic needs towards a mature structure of ambition, stable ideals, and values, and the engagement of inherent talents with societal and physical reality.

First method

- Ignore or actively shame a child's authentic initiatives. Do not mirror and display empathy for the child's "true self" and development as his or her own "centre of initiative".
- Make love highly conditional.
- Reward behaviour that supports the mother's image of the child she wants.
- Discourage contact with the father, thus keeping the child trapped in the dyad.

Second method

- Encourage (or fail to engage in optimal discouragement of) the child's grandiosity, egocentricity, and sense of entitlement – of being special. Parental narcissism extends to a view that their child must be subject to no limits.
- Combine this with a lack of development-nurturing "tough love".

Third method

- Subject the child to rejection and abuse – creating a sense of grievance and entitlement to recompense for past wrongs.
- The child has some area of talent around which the pathological grandiose self can form – for example, physical strength/ capacity for violence; good looks and charm; high intelligence.

Fourth method

- Produce a child with a temperament that impedes resolution of narcissism – such as ADHD.

The fourth method merits a little more elucidation. A key component of the neurobiology of ADHD is a deficit in the functioning of the frontal lobes, concerned with planning and with regulation of emotions and impulses. The frontal lobes may be considered a core part of the neurobiological underpinning of the Freudian ego functions that mediate between midbrain desires, emotions, and impulses and the realities of the external world. In ADHD, these functions are in deficit, resulting in impulsiveness, emotional dysregulation, and difficulties in sustaining attention and other executive functions. People with this condition have a greater than average need for selfobject responses from others to assist in emotional regulation and other ego functions. In the absence of these, the person's ego may "disintegrate" into panic and rage (Mollon, 2015).

It can be helpful to think of narcissism as having an imperative drive-like quality, which is particularly apparent in childhood. Thus, it falls into the category of impulses that are difficult for the child, and ADHD adult, to control and mediate along socially acceptable modes of expression. Grandiosity and demands for attention may remain childlike and unmediated. Those around the adult person with ADHD whose narcissism is unregulated may feel acute discomfort and embarrassment – and the person with the ADHD may even feel this as well, at the same time as being unable to inhibit the narcissistic display.

For the young child, the Freudian "primary process" prevails, consisting of a primacy of pleasure-seeking and a disregard of reality and of logic – a mode of functioning prevalent in dreams. During the course of development, the primary process is normally replaced to a large extent by the reality principle and secondary process, as the ego recognises the path to satisfaction requires taking account of reality, both physical and social, and that often inhibition of impulse and postponement of action are necessary for the eventual fulfilment of desire and achievement of goals. In the case of the person with ADHD, this development does not take place to its optimum degree, and the pleasure principle prevails beyond its phase-appropriate period. The narcissism of the primary process remains untamed. Grandiose illusions may persist, untroubled by logic and reality.

THE "FRAGILE SELF" MODEL OF NARCISSISTIC
DISTURBANCE

This was first proposed as a comprehensive model in *The Fragile Self* (Mollon, 1993), as a way of accounting for all the main characteristics of narcissism described by various authors, and also linking to the seven categories of the taxonomy of disturbances in the sense of self. Two stages are proposed, developmentally entwined but conceptually distinguished.

The first level of disturbance concerns failures of early communication and empathy, the non-mirroring mother (or other primary caregiver), and failure to develop a primal sense of efficacy (Mollon, 1985). Following Broucek (1979), it was proposed that the basis of the sense of self is the experience of efficacy, of having an effect on the world. Most fundamentally, it may be postulated (following similar suggestions by Bion, 1962, and Winnicott, 1960) that a crucial basis of the sense of efficacy is the ability to evoke a thoughtful emotional response in the mother. Such failures would also fall into the category of Kohut's (1971, 1977) account of deficits in selfobject responsiveness. They would also be expected to contribute to Winnicott's (1960) description of the "false self" that is formed when the mother substitutes her own gesture rather than responding to that of her child. Failures and deficits of this kind would seem likely to lead to disturbances particularly in category 2 of the taxonomy, the sense of agency, and category 4, the sense of organisation and coherence, which depends on the formation of a functional organisation with the selfobject, and also category 5, whereby there is excessive adaptation to the other at the expense of expression of self.

A second level of disturbance is the failure to progress from the dyadic relationship with the mother to the triadic or oedipal position which allows a place for the father. Lacan (1957) revealed how entry into the oedipal position may be associated with entry into the symbolic order, wherein the father (or the symbolic father) is perceived as a representative of the outside world, the "law", and the social order. Although the outward form of the oedipal situation may vary in different societies and cultures, the necessity to subject one's desires to the law (of society, kinship, family) is universal. Considered from this perspective, it can be seen that entry into the oedipal position (or failure to do so) can have profound psychic structural consequences.

In presenting Lacan's theorising, Lemaire (1977) writes:

> *Regardless of its variable forms, the oedipal phenomenon is, as a structure, a radical and universal transformation of the human being; it is the transition from a dual, immediate or mirror relationship to the mediate relationship proper to the symbolic, as opposed to the imaginary. (p. 78)*

Successful entry into the oedipal position, accepting the presence of rivals and generational differences and family structure, provides the child with a clearer sense of identity and of his or her place in the scheme of things, the social symbolic order. This allows a firmer separation of the images of self and other (category 1 of the taxonomy), a sense of lineage, of being part of a generational line (category 7), a recognition of interdependence of human beings within a family and society, as opposed to illusions of self-sufficiency (category 6).

Failure to achieve the triadic oedipal position may come about either because the father is absent, psychologically if not physically, failing in his paternal function of managing rivalries and boundaries (Diamond, 2018), or because the mother excludes the father and actively keeps the child within her domain of seduction and control – or a combination of the two. There can be a malignant alliance between a mother's and a child's wish omnipotently to abolish the father, thereby trapping the child in a developmental cul de sac from which it is difficult to escape. Of course, most mothers welcome the parenting partnership of the father or other figure carrying that function

– but occasionally we learn of a mother engaging in a deeply malign narcissistic process of progressively excluding and invalidating the father while she maintains increasing control over her children, who are thus trapped in the dyad. Without the psychic space provided by a triadic position, it is difficult for the child, and later the adult, to take a perspective on the self. He or she is trapped in the gaze and image provided by the mother – often a grandiose image (category 3 of the taxonomy), again expressing the mother's narcissism.

Freud (1923b) noted that the Oedipus complex occurs in both positive and negative forms – desiring exclusive possession of the mother and exclusion of the father, or possession of the father and exclusion of the mother – but that for both genders, the primary oedipal wish is to remain close to the mother and ward off the rival father. At the same time, the developmental necessity is that these wishes are gently thwarted.

With the banishment of the father from the psychic space, there can be a denial of the primal scene, the structuring schema of the parental intercourse as the origin of life (Laplanche & Pontalis, 1973. This fantasy is painful for the child because it signifies exclusion, and a relationship of the parents prior to his or her existence. Moreover, the nature of adult sexuality is inherently perplexing, frightening, and humiliating for the child (Mollon, 2005a). In some patients with disabling narcissistic disturbance, the primal scene is foreclosed – either through the collusion of the mother who wishes to feel she produced her child all by herself, or because the fantasy model is too violent, the parents seen as coming together in a purely destructive way. With the abortion of the primal scene, there is a psychic gap where the father and the schema of a parental relationship should be – leaving the child and adult with a deep puzzlement about identity and origins (category 7 of the taxonomy).

Peter Hildebrand (personal communication) suggested there may be a further primal fantasy corresponding to death and endings, juxtaposed to that of origins. Both origins and death function as limits to the twin grandiose fantasies of, first, to have created oneself, owing nothing to anyone, and second, to go on forever – death being the ultimate narcissistic insult.

Most of Kohut's clinical illustrations are consistent with the model outlined here and demonstrate a crucial role of the father in narcissistic disturbance, alongside failures in the early mirroring relationship with the mother (see the detailed analysis of these in Mollon, 1993). The father's role in facilitating the child's separation from the mother is apparent in Kohut's cases, but is not emphasised in Kohut's own theorising.

CLINICAL ILLUSTRATION OF THE TWO-STAGE MODEL

Mr J was a singer and dancer in his thirties. He was loud and flamboyant, but underneath his confident persona his despair, helplessness, and rage were apparent. Although achieving some success in his career, he was recurrently sabotaging of this in a variety of ways. For example, he might fail to turn up for work, or have rows with a director (particularly if female), or go on drinking binges. His relationships with women and sexual activities were pervaded by sadomasochism, and fears of being controlled and possessed. Although capable of kindness and warmth, he seemed to have little ability for true empathy. Despite his obvious intelligence, he appeared to lack a capacity for introspection, insight, and self-awareness. His inner awareness of his own emotions seemed absent, although he could successfully mimic their outward expression. He was clearly unhappy in both his relationships and his work, but was unable to say what he desired instead. When first seen for psychotherapy, he wanted to know what the plan was to shape, correct, or improve his personality. The idea of psychotherapy as a process of self-exploration seemed to him both puzzling and alarming. It was as if he expected to be directed or choreographed, and continually monitored – an idea that also made him enraged.

The background was that Mr J had grown up as an only child, close to his doting but controlling mother, but with relatively little contact with his father, a reclusive sculptor. His mother had always wanted him to be on stage and had greatly encouraged and praised his performances. However, he had clearly experienced her as somewhat dominant and perhaps feminising, discouraging more boyish pursuits. He had been sent to a small private school, specialising in arts and performance, which he had quite enjoyed whilst also engaging in periodic acts of delinquency that nearly resulted in his expulsion.

He reported two early memories. One was of his enjoyment of singing for his mother while standing on a table, imagining a big audience. The other was of setting a trap of string in his father's studio, with the fantasy that his father would trip over it and have to go to hospital and then he could marry his mother – he recalled consciously that he had been "madly in love with my mother and wanted my father to go away". Both memories seemed to be from around the age of four or five. He felt his mother had encouraged his feeling that the two of them were the primary couple, and his father the occasional intruder.

It was apparent that Mr J's development had been hijacked by his mother's image of the performing child she wanted. While the closeness to his mother had been gratifying, it also meant his developmental opportunities to explore his own desires and interests had been relatively foreclosed. His adaptation to, and identification with, his mother's image of him had created a grandiose false self – one which in his rage he unconsciously wished to destroy.

In the transference, he initially viewed the therapist as a (maternal) figure to please. Gradually, his rage-fuelled wish to rebel emerged into clearer focus, along with his search for a paternal response.

One morning he arrived at the clinic a little earlier than the psychotherapist, and this time refused the usual convention of sitting in the waiting room, instead insisting on going straight up to the

therapist's room. When the therapist subsequently enquired what had been going through Mr J's
mind when he refused the receptionist's direction
to sit in the waiting room until called, he thought
for a few seconds and then said, with some passion,
that at that moment the middle-aged receptionist
had represented every woman who had told him
what to do, beginning with his mother! His second
thought was of remembering his mother's frequent
injunction not to bother his father by going into
his room. This expression of true transference was
a vivid revelation of the underlying developmental dynamics of his narcissistic disturbance – the
captivation by the image in his mother's mind of
the kind of boy she wanted, and mutual collusion
to exclude the father.

During the process of psychotherapy, Mr J
became calmer, quieter, more aware of his true
feelings, including his rage towards his mother,
and his longing for paternal relationships and in-
terventions. He developed an idealising selfobject
transference towards the male therapist, and also

towards a male martial arts instructor – indicating strivings to merge with perceived qualities of wisdom, calm, and centred masculinity – thus following a typical reparative developmental pathway described by Kohut (1971, 1977). His interests shifted towards his own creativity, drawing upon deeper and more authentic psychic currents. Following the therapy, he was less self-destructive and had a very successful career.

THE STORY OF ECHO AND NARCISSUS

The classic myth of Narcissus and Echo, as told by Ovid (Vinge, 1967) contains all the key ingredients of narcissistic disturbance.

Narcissus is born of a violent "primal scene", as the nymph Liriope is raped by the river god Cephisus. There is no continuing parental couple and no father available to Narcissus.

His origins are preceded by the pronouncement by Tiresias that he should not know himself and should remain in ignorance of who he is and where he comes from. Narcissus does indeed become trapped in his incapacity to recognise himself. He is captivated by the image of himself in the pool, falls in love with it, is unable to move, and subsequently dies.

Narcissus is "narcissistic" – aloof, spurning his admirers' attentions, with "pride so cold that no youth, no maiden touched his heart". He is afraid of being exploited or possessed, dismissing Echo's approach with the words, "Hands off! Embrace me not! May I die before I give you power over me!" His mother Liriope also appears to have been narcissistic – Vinge (1967) describes Narcissus as "proud and unapproachable as his mother was", suggesting that she may have been unresponsive to Narcissus, other than perhaps admiring his beauty.

Narcissus is desired, yet is completely unobtainable and unreachable, as if wishing to retain all his desirable qualities for himself. A spurned lover utters a curse, granted by the god Nemesis, that "he himself love and not gain the thing he loves".

The story is pervaded by envy, sadism, and

masochism. Narcissus treats his admirers sadistically, sending one suitor a sword with which to kill himself (Graves, 1955). By contrast, Echo is masochistically enslaved to Narcissus, unable to take any part or initiative in the dialogue, restricted to the role of auditory mirror. Narcissus and Echo are sadist and masochist trapped with each other. They are both captivated by image and illusion.

The following themes are apparent in the myth:

- Illusion and captivation by a deceptive image
- A lack of self-knowledge and knowledge of origins – no sense of lineage
- A lack of knowledge of the other – and lack of desire for such knowledge
- Being trapped in the functions of reflection and mirroring – the malign variant of the selfobject
- Sadomasochism – Echo's masochistic fidelity to Narcissus's sadism
- The fear of being possessed and taken over

- Vanity and pride – and a turning away from relatedness to others
- Envy provoked by narcissism – and narcissism as a defence against envy
- The dangers of self-absorption and illusion – a developmental cul de sac and death
- Origins in a violent primal scene and the absence of a continuing parental couple.

Borderline states

The term "borderline personality disorder" (BPD) is easy to misunderstand. The name can suggest a mild condition that is on the borderline of being a personality disorder. In reality, of course, it can denote sometimes extremely severe disturbances of personality. In origin, the "borderline" referred to states of mind and personality that appeared at the border of neurosis and psychosis.

The concept became popular during the late 1970s and 1980s. Thus, Solomon, Lang, and Grotstein (1987) wrote:

The concept of a borderline entity stems from several disciplines. Psychoanalysts and psychiatrists seem to have discovered it independently. From hospital practice with seriously disturbed patients, as well as from an increasing number of reports on nonhospitalized but very disturbed patients, a picture gradually emerged of a puzzling group of patients who sometimes appeared psychotic, although they did not either clearly fit the deteriorative aspects of schizophrenia or follow the clinical course of affective illness. On the other hand, analytically oriented clinicians were beginning to notice a group of patients who at first appeared to be neurotic, but in time exhibited significant and puzzling differences in character structure, symptomatology, and clinical course. These patients seemed "sicker", their pathology far more primitive, and their therapeutic course much stormier that the original diagnostic impressions had predicted. (p. 3)

Currently, such conditions seem prevalent, with many patients of psychiatric services presenting with combinations of chaotic behaviours involving self-harm, mood disorders, extreme unmanageable anxiety, and misuse of drugs and alcohol. The more circumscribed "neuroses" of the past seem less common, as do the classic presentations of schizophrenia. This suggests that mental health disorders are to some extent culturally shaped, and perhaps also that our society has become more chaotic and disordered. Each person, and perhaps each society and culture, has evolved its own way of expressing disturbance and emotional pain.

There have been a number of precursors of the concept of borderline personality disorder: ambulatory schizophrenias (Zilboorg, 1941); "as if" personalities (Deutsch, (1942); pseudoneurotic schizophrenia (Hoch & Polatin, 1949); borderline states (Knight, 1953; Robbins, 1956); severe ego distortions (Gitelson, 1958); preschizophrenic personality structure (Rapaport, Schafer, & Gill,

1945); psychotic characters (Frosch, 1964). The more modern concept became greatly popularised by Kernberg's landmark book *Borderline Conditions and Pathological Narcissism* (1975), in which he conceptualised both borderline and narcissistic conditions through an amalgamation of Kleinian perspectives on primitive defences of projection and splitting, and American psychoanalytic ego psychology, as developed by Hartman (1964), Jacobson (1965), and others. Essentially, Kernberg viewed the borderline state as a variant of the Kleinian paranoid-schizoid position (Klein, 1946).

Adolph Stern (1938) wrote the first paper on such conditions: "Psychoanalytic Investigation of and Therapy in the Borderline Group of Neuroses". Here he described a variety of characteristics, including narcissistic phenomena. He wrote of the patients' "inordinate sensitivity", "inferiority feelings", insecurity and anxiety, reliance on projective mechanisms, and tendency towards "psychic bleeding", whereby they would show little resilience but would react to painful experiences by "going down in a heap", emotionally "bleeding". Regarding the early family environment, Stern described the parents as non-protective, neglectful, and often cruel, incorporating the child into their own sadomasochistic emotional atmosphere. The child was not allowed to be free to pursue his or her autonomous development and wider relationships. Wolberg (1982) found this early paper captured important qualities of these borderline mental states, noting:

> *My observation is that parents who have a disturbed, tumultuous home keep the child from forming adequate relations with peers because of their paranoid feelings and their need to hold on to and use the children as projective objects. These parents often have a fear of strangers and of people invading the privacy of their sadomasochistic defensive system. The problems of the parents frustrate the child in finding companions and keep him in the sadomasochistic bind. (p. 46)*

A common feature of those who are given a diagnosis of BPD is an inconsistent presentation, sometimes calm and thoughtful and at other times volatile and chaotic. A second feature is that the work with the client turns out to be complex and difficult. Deep anxieties and dysfunctional beliefs powerfully impede progress.

In many ways, BPD states are like narcissistic disorders without the stabilising narcissistic structure – or perhaps we might say they are like a destabilised narcissistic disorder. It appears that the primitive child psyche has not been harnessed to social reality through the consistent availability of development-facilitating and emotion-regulating selfobject responses from the caregivers. Moreover, this primitive, incoherent, and unregulated state has not coalesced around a stable narcissistic structure of a pathological grandiose self.

For Kohut (1971), borderline states involved a regression to the state of a fragmented self. He considered that the two developmental lines of narcissism, the grandiose self and the idealised object, when transmuted by phase-appropriate empathic responses from the selfobject environment, gave rise to a stable structure of self. This healthy stable structure consisted of enduring ambitions, ideals, connected to real talents and skills. From a theoretical position combining Kleinian and American ego-psychological frameworks, Kernberg (1975) described how narcissistic development may proceed to a *pathological* but *stable* self-structure – the pathological grandiose self, consisting of a fusion of the images of the ideal self, the ideal object, and the actual self. Both theorists, although presenting very different perspectives, indicate that narcissistic developments, healthy and pathological, can provide escape from the early state of the fragmented self. Lacan (1937) also described developmental processes whereby identification with an image of the self, in the "mirror stage", provided a new state of coherence in place of the earlier fragmented self. This insight is also implied in Freud's (1914c) account, where the emergence of narcissism, a cathexis of the ego, replaces an earlier more fragmented state of autoerotism in which different sensory regions of the body are cathected. Kohut and Lacan, each in very different ways, indicated that the potential regression to the state of the fragmented self could evoke intense and overwhelming anxiety.

Those diagnosed with BPD often present childhood histories of exposure to chaotic or abusive early family environments (Bateman & Fonagy, 2004), sometimes including sexual abuse, or receiving or witnessing physical violence. Intense and overwhelming emotions would be a frequent occurrence, along with many adverse experiences that could not be managed or processed. As a result, the child and adolescent would develop a range of pathological methods of regulating emotion.

BPD states tend to display very starkly the intense approach-avoidance conflicts that can arise from deficiencies or malformations of the original caregiver matrix. While the more explicitly narcissistic disorders are organised around *pathology of the self* (as a structure), in BPD conditions it is these intense conflicts in *relationships with others* that come into focus, along with attempts to manage the accompanying overwhelming emotions, often by desperately attempting to prevent different parts of the mind from coming into association (Glasser, 1992; Green, 2000). These psychic struggles are often thought of as narcissistic, insofar as they may involve libidinal withdrawal and are organised against the perceived dangers of relationships that are nevertheless strongly desired (Kreisman, & Straus, 1989). There may be attempts to overcome a sense of separation and potential abandonment by seeking to intrude upon, possess, or create a state of oneness with the other, or, by contrast, to obliterate desire and life itself (Green, 2001, 2002). They arise because early in the person's life the attachment relationship was both needed, as a source of love and life, and feared, as a source of pain, danger, and potential annihilation. Thus, in one of her papers on narcissism, Perelberg (2004) states: "For all the patients discussed in my paper, achieving both trust in the object and separation from the object might be, perhaps, the most unattainable task. For each of these patients the body of the mother was not experienced as a home, a safe place that allowed for exploration and creativity" (p. 1077). In such a position, the child is caught in a limbo, trapped indeed on a *border*, neither able fully to relate nor be creatively alone – and not able to regulate and manage emotions. It is possible then to see that narcissistic and borderline disturbances are two sides of the same coin, one displaying pathology of the self and the other pathology of relationships, but both rooted in failures of the early selfobject provision.

Those who are given a diagnosis of BPD often convey a sense of having no "floor" or safe ground on which their personality is built, experiencing a terror of falling, of descending into a chasm, and of disintegrating. Perhaps such fears are primal and universal, but in more favourable conditions, optimal experiences of soothing by the selfobject responses of caregivers help to alleviate these and facilitate a foundation of security and stable self-structure. This is missing for those with BPD. The dreaded state of collapse may also be interwoven with intense toxic shame, and suicidal striving (Mollon, 2002; West, 2016). Shame is, in its most extreme and fundamental form, a state of utter rejection and of feeling not fit to be part of the human group.

Recognising the emotional chaos and unmanageable impulses that such people are struggling with, an evolving modern perspective sees borderline conditions as disorders of affect-regulation or self-regulation. Thus, Grotstein (1987) commented:

> *I propose the concept of disorders of self-regulation as an alternative method of understanding psychopathology in general and the psychopathology of the borderline in particular ... designates a breakdown of the regulation of bodily and psychic states such as states of arousal, attention, sleep,*

*wakefulness, self-esteem, affects, needs
… [with] secondary symptoms and syn-
dromes that follow in train as the organism
seeks to compensate for this dysregulation.
(pp. 348–349)*

Similarly, Allan Schore (1994) conceptualised BPD within his developing neurobiology of
affect-regulation:

*Borderline personalities experience rapid-
ly shifting states, and this state transition
may be sudden and traumatic. Phenome-
nologically it is experienced as a precipitous
entrance into a shame-associated chaotic
state, fascinatingly described by Grotstein
… as a descent into a "black hole" … I understand these events to represent a major
regulatory failure that triggers a rapid psy-
chobiological state transition, an implosion
– a sudden shift from a high energy state to
a parasympathetic low energy state … a*

sudden dramatic shift from extreme hy-peractivity to extreme hypoactivity of the orbitofrontal cortex ... (p. 421)

Modern attachment theorists, such as Fonagy and colleagues (Allen, Fonagy, & Bateman, 2008) view BPD through the lens of disorganised attachment, wherein chaotic early environments prevent affect-regulation and mentalisation, and give rise to internal working models in which relational trust and intimacy are perceived as dangerous. Abandonment is a core fear. The perception of other people's minds, their emotions and motives, are felt to be too frightening to tolerate, and so mentalising is shut down. Moreover, the person's own potential emotions are feared to be too intense and destabilising, and so these too are shut down. Allen, Fonagy, and Bateman (2008) conclude: "We believe that the central factor that predisposes the child to BPD is a family environment that discourages coherent discourse concerning mental states" (p. 274).

A key factor that is very often missed in considerations of BPD is the role of ADHD as a central neurobiological core around which all the expressions of the borderline picture are organised (Mollon, 2015). Since the BPD phenomena can present such a prominent picture, the core of ADHD is often missed. However, ADHD is a clinical picture emerging from the interaction of a particular neurobiological template and a family environment. With deficient frontal lobes, there is impaired executive functioning, and an enhanced need for external assistance with ego functions and selfobject responses of empathy for soothing. The person with ADHD lives on the edge of chaos – of disintegration. When the external selfobject assistance with ego functions and soothing fails, the person may indeed psychologically disintegrate and be overwhelmed with anxiety, panic, and rage – and may resort to a variety of dysfunctional attempts to manage these states and to force others to provide assistance. These dysfunctional strategies may include violence, self-harm, or abuse of drugs or alcohol. The person may be further overwhelmed and traumatised by his or her own emotions and dysfunctional coping strategies – creating a spiralling state of chaos that sucks the individual and those associated with him or her into a terrifying black hole.

There is overlap between some of the expressions of ADHD and those of trauma. Moreover, people who have ADHD are more inclined to experience trauma, for broadly two reasons: first, they are more impulsive and inclined towards risk-taking and are accident-prone; second, they may have a highly adverse effect on their interpersonal environment, driving others in their family to extreme irritation and potential rage.

MISUSE OF THE DIAGNOSIS OF BPD AND OTHER PERSONALITY DISORDERS

In the British NHS currently, the computerised clinical notes system requires every patient to be given a diagnosis, in order to be assigned to a care pathway. These processes of categorisation have financial implications. Thus, diagnosis is applied at least as much for business as for clinical reasons. As a result, all patients receive a copy of any letters written about them (another NHS requirement), which displays their official diagnosis prominently at the top of the page along with their other key signifiers of name, address, and date of birth.

What does it mean for a patient to read that they are categorised with such a label as "borderline personality disorder"? For some, it appears to provide some relief – a sense of fitting in somewhere, of having a diagnosis that means their suffering and behaviour can somehow be understood and perhaps cured. For others, it is profoundly alienating, offering an identification with a false image, an illusion, and a form of words that threatens to define their life. In many instances it functions as an imposed identity, whereby the clinical system says, in effect, "Regardless of how you experience yourself, we are going to see you as this diagnosis". No matter how humane and thoughtful the individual clinician might be, the clinical system as a whole, with its computerised records and financially governed care pathways, does impose a false identity on many psychiatric service users.

A key point to keep in mind is that the diagnosis of any personality disorder is not strictly equivalent to other forms of medical diagnosis, although the fact that it is called a diagnosis gives the illusion of such equivalence. In the case of a physical illness, there is a set of symptoms, from which a doctor diagnoses an underlying illness, sometimes with the aid of various kinds of medical tests. The symptoms are *indicators* of the underlying illness, but the symptoms themselves do not comprise the entire illness. In the case of a "diagnosis" such as BPD (and indeed many mental health conditions) there are symptoms but there is no underlying condition to which they point. The symptoms comprise the entire illness. If we were to ask, "Why does Sally experience mood swings, self-harm, and misuse alcohol?" the answer would be "Because she has a borderline personality disorder" – but if we ask "How do you know she has a borderline personality disorder?" the answer would be "Because she experiences mood swings, self-harm, and misuses alcohol". The "diagnosis" is not really a diagnosis, so much as a convenient category for describing a certain set of commonly co-occurring experiences and behaviours.

The preceding paragraph is not true in every instance. For example, it might be possible to say that a particular patient displays the characteristics of BPD, but there is no history of extensive childhood abuse or dysfunctional family, and that this points to a likely underlying condition of ADHD. Similarly, a sophisticated psychoanalytic clinician might make an inference from a pattern of BPD behaviour to an underlying form of psychic structure and constellation of particular mental defences. In both these instances, the reference to a personality disorder would have genuine diagnostic significance – it would be a signifier of an underlying condition. In most psychiatric practice, this is not the case.

Although the diagnostic criteria of the American Diagnostic and Statistical Manual of Mental Disorders are presented as if scientifically valid, Bradley and colleagues (Bradley, Conklin, & Westen, 2007) note problems with the three areas of heterogeneity of symptom presentation, categorical diagnosis, and excessive comorbidity with other disorders: "With respect to heterogeneity, a patient can receive the BPD diagnosis in over 150 different ways based on varying combinations of the nine criteria for the disorder ... Put another way, two patients may be diagnosed with BPD while sharing only one symptom in common" (p. 170). They argue also that most research on personality disorders favours the concept of dimensions of characteristics rather than clear categories, and shows considerable overlap between the diagnostic categories.

The sloppy logic of diagnoses of personality disorder, particularly BPD, can have extremely adverse consequences when used in legal contexts, such as family courts where decisions about the placing of children are considered. I have come across a number of distressing instances of mothers having acquired at some point in their history a diagnosis of borderline personality disorder. Regardless of the mother's current functioning, this diagnostic label has shaped legal thinking about her fitness to look after her children. If she functions well at present, this is discounted because she has this "illness" and may relapse. Since it is argued that psychotherapeutic treatment of BPD takes years of intensive work, the mother is viewed as incapable of recovering within the timescale of the child's needs. Another variant is to assume that if a person has this diagnosis, he or she must have suffered childhood sexual abuse, which then must be addressed in psychotherapy, which again will (it is said) take years. Yet another common form of faulty reasoning is to say that because this woman has this "diagnosis", she must have dialectical behaviour therapy, since that is a recommended treatment – if this is not available, then she will not be able to function well as a mother. All these forms of logical slippage can be catastrophically damaging for the woman concerned and her children – and for the thoughtful clinicians among us they are also profoundly embarrassing, particularly when we find psychiatrists or psychologists colluding with this madness.

THOUGHTS ON HELPFUL ASPECTS OF PSYCHOTHERAPY WITH NARCISSISTIC AND BORDERLINE STATES

Although psychoanalysis informs all my work, there are certain contemporary fashions of technique and style that I have come to feel are unhelpful (Mollon, 2014). An aloof psychoanalytic stance does not help the client to feel at ease, does not facilitate an atmosphere of trust and exploration, and tends to evoke or exacerbate feelings of shame (Mollon, 2002); ordinary human warmth and friendliness, albeit expressed with restraint and respect for boundaries, are more helpful.

An exclusive or excessive emphasis on "transference" can also be very unhelpful (Bollas, 2007;

Mollon, 2011, 2014a). Freud's stance of focusing on transference only when it appears clearly, and treating it as an illusion, allows a more collaborative and constructive mode of work. For example, Freud (1920g) wrote, "It has been the physician's endeavour to keep this transference neurosis within the narrowest limits: to force as much as possible into the channel of memory and to allow as little as possible to emerge as repetition" (p. 18), and (1940a), "It is the analyst's task constantly to tear the patient out of his menacing illusion and to show him again and again that what he takes to be new real life is a reflection of the past" (p. 177). Although it must be addressed when it arises, seeking out transference, and dwelling on it, tends to evoke more of it and can provoke regression. Moreover, it can encourage a harmful illusion that the relationship with the therapist or analyst will somehow make up for the failings and injuries of the childhood past.

With patients who have experienced extremely malign early environments, pervaded by trauma, abuse, and cruelty, an undue focus on transference can be frankly dangerous. The reason is that, in the logic of transference, the therapist will at some point be seen as having qualities of the worst figures of childhood (Mollon, 2001b). Some forms of extreme interpersonal trauma simply cannot be contained safely within the transference illusion, and the result is a transference *psychosis*. A common but paradoxical transference-based anxiety can arise when the patient begins to trust the therapist more, since this may run counter to a belief that trust is dangerous and that it is not safe to feel safe (Mollon, 1996).

I have found that a friendly and workman-like stance of being a companion and guide in the patient's exploration of his or her own mind and history is more helpful than a focus on transference. The therapist's task is to facilitate the exploration, and at times to explain what might be going on, since the awareness and understanding of some phenomena are beyond the reach of introspection. In this work, the conveying of empathy is important – but this is not a superficial comment-ing on surface emotions but a searching out of the deep qualities of a person's experience, dilemmas, struggles, and emotional pain and terror. The meta message is something like "Yes, life is hard, confus-ing, often frightening, sometimes evoking despair – and we all make a mess of it – but I am here alongside you temporarily in this journey."

Areas of experience to focus on will include all the pains and suffering of narcissism and narcissis-tic wounds, as well as the terrors of disintegration. Each client will have suffered ways in which her or his early psychological development was com-promised or foreclosed – and awareness of these evokes sadness, and at times rage.

Throughout the work, it is important not to assume that we know or understand the client, even though we may strive to do so. If we believe we have reached some understanding, this may be true for a moment, but quickly becomes false if we cling to it. What was true in the previous session may not be true today. If there is a "true" self, it is always an emerging unknown self. I recommend a stance of viewing the client as a sacred unknown being – if we are patient and respectful, he or she may come to reveal something of who they are. In this process, we help them in their own discovery.

As with the human species as a whole, the clients and patients we see are afflicted by the alienating captivation by images, words, and the entire symbolic network in which we dwell. Jacques Lacan emphasised how entry into the symbolic realm of language and language-like structures and processes, a pre-existing order that shapes, defines, and locates the human subject, marked our species as unique among the inhabitants of the earth. For Lacan, it is the entry into the register of language that creates a fundamental break from the natural order of the "real". Much of human life exists within a matrix of symbols, signs, and signifiers – whether these be words (written or spoken), gestures, rules of the road, the law, the personal coordinates of name, date, and place of birth, or the semiotics of fashion, personal belongings, and signifiers of status. Recent prominent protests concerning climate change have prompted me to extend Lacan's concept of the symbolic to include all the ways in which energy, mostly derived from burning fossil fuels, has been used to transform the "real" into the fabric and equipment of modern life. This transformation of the real has created an environment radically severed from that inhabited by all other species on the planet. We rarely encounter the "real" of the physical and natural world. In an urban environment, almost all that we encounter during our day is a transformation of the real, which has been incorporated into the symbolic. The raw material of the real has been transformed by the burning of fossil fuels and made part of the symbolic – into materials and objects that not only have function but also many social meanings. In our contemporary culture, this expanded symbolic register is entwined with that of the image, this realm of the imaginary greatly enhanced and exaggerated by the dominance of social media, the constant posting of images, and the amount of time spent looking at images on screens. For these reasons, some degree of escape from the symbolic and imaginary registers (Faber, 2013), and reconnection with the "real" may be essential for mental health. Mindfulness meditation, physical exercise, gardening, or walking among trees, plants, and wildlife, and many traditional forms of psychiatric occupational therapy, are examples of activities that may have a wholesome effect.

There can also be much value in gently encouraging the patient to become less preoccupied with the self-image – pointing to its illusory nature – and assisting him or her in focusing on external tasks and real work. Helping the person to consider the question of her or his true desires and goals, obscured by the image, can also be a seemingly simple yet profoundly liberating function of the psychotherapist.

Finally, I must confess that although "psychoanalyst" remains a core part of my own identity, my clinical practice has come to include much that is beyond that framework – in particular, the various modalities known generically as "energy psychology" (Mollon, 2005b, 2008, 2014b). These involve guiding clients to work with their own body's energy system concurrently with addressing the flow of emotion and information in their mind. All the content of psychoanalysis remains highly relevant – but the process flows more easily and deeply when combined with acupoint tapping.

REFERENCES

Allen, J. G., Fonagy, P., & Bateman, A. W. (2008). *Mentalizing in Clinical Practice*. Arlington, VA: American Psychiatric Publishing.

Balint, M. (1968). *The Basic Fault*. London: Tavistock.

Bancroft, L. (2002). *Why Does He Do That?: Inside the Minds of Angry and Controlling Men*. New York: Berkley, 2003.

Bateman, A., & Fonagy, P. (2004). *Psychotherapy for Borderline Personality Disorder. Mentalization-Based Treatment*. Oxford. Oxford University Press.

Bernardi, R., & Eidlin, M. (2018). Thin-skinned or vulnerable narcissism and thick-skinned or grandiose narcissism: similarities and differences. *International Journal of Psychoanalysis*, 99(2): 291–313.

Bernstein, J. (2013). Current trends in the treatment of narcissism: Spotnitz, Kohut, Kernberg. *Modern Psychoanalysis*, 38(1): 25–49.

Bion, W. R. (1962). *Learning from Experience*. London. Heinemann. [Reprinted London: Karnac, 1984.]

Bion, W. R. (1965). *Transformations*. London. Heinemann. [Reprinted London: Karnac, 1984.]

Bogat, G. A., Garcia, A. M., & Levendosky, A. A. (2013). Assessment and psychotherapy with women experiencing intimate partner violence: integrating research and practice. *Psychodynamic Psychiatry*, 41(2): 189–217.

Bollas, C. (2007). On transference interpretation as a resistance to free-association. Chapter 5 in *The Freudian Moment*. London: Karnac.

Borgogno, F. (2016). Narcissism, psychic recognition, and affective validation: A homage to the "later Rosenfeld". *International Forum of Psychoanalysis*, 25(4): 249–256.

Bradley, R., Conklin, C. Z., & Westen, D. (2007). Borderline person-

References

ality disorder. Chapter 7 in O'Donohue, W., Fowler, K. A., & Lilienfeld, S. O. (Eds.), *Personality Disorders.Toward the DSM-V* (pp. 167–201). London: Sage.

Broucek, F. (1979). Efficacy in infancy: a review of some experimental studies and their possible implications for clinical theory. *International Journal of Psychoanalysis*, 60: 311–316.

Coffman, D. (2017). Normal Narcissism in the Age of Trump: The Americanization of Narcissism by E. Lunbeck (Cambridge, MA: Harvard University Press). *Psychoanalysis and History*, 19(3): 407–413.

Deutsch, H. (1942). Some forms of emotional disturbance and their relationship to schizophrenia. *Psychoanalytic Quarterly*, 11: 301–321.

Diamond, M. J. (2018). When fathering fails: violence, narcissism, and the father function in ancient tales and clinical analysis. *Journal of the American Psychoanalytic Association*, 66(1): 7–40.

Faber, M. D. (2013). *The Withdrawal of Human Projection. Separating from the Symbolic Order*. New York: Library of Social Science.

Freud, S. (1911b). *Formulations on the two principles of mental functioning. S. E., 12*. London: Hogarth.

Freud, S. (1914c). *On narcissism: an introduction. S. E., 14*. London: Hogarth.

Freud, S. (1920g). *Beyond the Pleasure Principle. S. E., 18*. London: Hogarth.

Freud, S. (1921c). *Group Psychology and the Analysis of the Ego. S. E., 18*. London: Hogarth.

Freud, S. (1923b). *The Ego and the Id. S. E., 19*. London: Hogarth.

Freud, S. (1940a). *An Outline of Psycho-analysis. S. E., 23*. London: Hogarth.

Frosch, J. (1964). The psychotic character. *Psychiatric Quarterly*, 38: 81–96.

Gear, M. C., Hill, M. A., & Liendo, E. L. (1981). *Working Through Narcissism: Treating its Sado-Masochistic Structure*. New York: Jason Aronson.

Gear, M. C., Liendo, E. C., & Scott, L. L. (1983). *Patients and Agents. Transference-Countertransference in Therapy.* New York: Jason Aronson.

Gitelson, M. (1958). On ego distortion. *International Journal of Psychoanalysis*, 39: 245–257.

Glasser, M. (1992). Problems in the psychoanalysis of certain narcissistic disorders. *International Journal of Psychoanalysis*, 73: 493–503.

Graves, R. (1955). *The Greek Myths.* London: Penguin.

Green, A. (2000). The central phobic position: a new formulation of the free association method. *International Journal of Psychoanalysis*, 81(3): 429–451.

Green, A. (2001). *Life Narcissism, Death Narcissism.* A. Weller (Trans.). London: Free Association.

Green, A. (2002). A dual conception of narcissism: positive and negative organization. *Psychoanalytic Quarterly*, 71: 631–649.

Greenberg, D. E. (2016). A review of Traumatic Narcissism: Relational Systems of Subjugation by Daniel Shaw (New York: Routledge, 2014, 192 pp.). *Contemporary Psychoanalysis*, 52(1): 130–143.

Greenwald, A. G. (1980). The totalitarian ego: fabrication and revision of personal history. *American Psychology*, 35: 603–608.

Groddeck, G. (1929). *The Unknown Self.* London: Daniel.

Grotstein, J. S. (1981). *Splitting and Projective Identification.* New York: Jason Aronson.

Grotstein, J. S. (1987). The borderline as a disorder of self-regulation. In: J. S. Grotstein, M. F. Solomon, & J. A. Lang (Eds.), *The Borderline Patient. Emerging Concepts in Diagnosis, Psychodynamics, and Treatment* (pp. 347–383). Hillsdale, NJ: The Analytic Press.

Hartmann, H. (1964). *Essays on Ego Psychology.* New York: International Universities Press.

Hoch, P. H., & Polatin, P. (1949). Pseudoneurotic forms of schizophrenia. *Psychiatric Quarterly*, 23: 248–276.

Home Office (2015). Controlling or coercive behaviour in an

intimate or family relationship. www.gov.uk/government/publications/statutory-guidance-framework-controlling-or-co-ercive-behaviour-in-an-intimate-or-family-relationship.

Jacobson, E. (1965). *The Self and the Object World*. London: Hogarth.

Jacobson, E. (1971). *Depression. Comparative Studies of Normal, Neurotic, and Psychotic Conditions.* New York: International Universities Press.

Kalshed, D. (1996). *The Inner World of Trauma. Archetypal Defenses of the Personal Spirit*. London: Routledge.

Kernberg, O. (1975). *Borderline Conditions and Pathological Narcissism*. New York: Jason Aronson.

Klein, M. (1946). Notes on some schizoid mechanisms. In: *Envy and Gratitude: The Writings of Melanie Klein, III*. London, Hogarth, 1975.

Knight, R. P. (1953). Borderline states. *Bulletin of the Menninger Clinic,* 17: 1–12.

Koenigsberg, R. (2009). *Nations Have the Right to Kill: Hitler, the Holocaust and War.* New York: Library of Social Science.

Kohut, H. (1966). Forms and transformations of narcissism. *Journal of the American Psychoanalytic Association*, 14: 243–272. [Reprinted in *The Search for the Self: Selected Writings of Heinz Kohut, 1950-1978, 1*. New York: International Universities Press, 1978.

Kohut, H. (1971). *The Analysis of the Self: A Systematic Approach to the Psychoanalytic Treatment of Narcissistic Personality Disorders.* New York: International Universities Press.

Kohut, H. (1972). Thoughts on narcissism and narcissistic rage. *Psychoanalytic Study of the Child*, 27: 360–400. Reprinted in *The Search for the Self: Selected Writings of Heinz Kohut, 1950-1978, 2*. New York: International Universities Press, 1978.

Kohut, H. (1977). *The Restoration of the Self*. New York: International Universities Press.

Kohut, H. (1979). The two analyses of Mr Z. *International Journal of Psychoanalysis*, 60: 3–27. Reprinted in *The Search for the*

Self: Selected Writings of Heinz Kohut, 4. New York: International Universities Press, 1991.

Kohut, H. (1983). Selected problems of self psychological theory. In: J. Litchenberg & S. Kaplan (Eds.), *Reflections on Self Psychology.* Hillsdale, NJ: The Analytic Press.

Kohut, H. (1984). *How Does Analysis Cure?* Chicago, IL: University of Chicago Press.

Kohut, H. (1990). On courage. Chapter 3, in *The Search for the Self: Selected Writings of Heinz Kohut, 3.* New York: International Universities Press.

Kohut, H. (1996). *The Chicago Institute Lectures.* P. Tolpin & M. Tolpin (Eds.). Hillsdale, NJ: The Analytic Press.

Kreisman, J. J., & Straus, H. (1989). *I Hate You – Don't Leave Me: Understanding the Borderline Personality.* New York: Perigree, 2010.

Lacan, J. (1937). The looking glass phase. *International Journal of Psychoanalysis,* 18. Reprinted as *"The mirror stage as formative of the function of the I."* In: Ecrits. London: Tavistock, 1977.

Lacan, J. (1956). The imaginary dissolution. Reprinted in J.-A. Miller (Ed.), *The Psychoses. The Seminar of Jacques Lacan. Book III,* 1955-1956. New York: W. W. Norton, 1993.

Lacan, J. (1957). On a question preliminary to any possible treatment of psychosis. In: *Ecrits.* London: Tavistock, 1977.

Lacan, J. (2013). *On the Names-of-the-Father (talks from 1953 and 1963).* Cambridge: Polity Press.

Laplanche, J., & Pontalis, J. B. (1973). *The Language of Psychoanalysis.* London: Hogarth.

Leader, D. (2012). *What is Madness?* London: Penguin.

Lemaire, A. (1977). *Jacques Lacan.* London: Routledge.

Lynch, S. M. (2013). Not good enough and on a tether: exploring how violent relationships impact women's sense of self. *Psychodynamic Psychiatry,* 41(2): 219–246.

Masterson, J. F., & Rinsley, D. B. (1980). The borderline syndrome. The role of the mother in the genesis and psychic structure of the borderline personality. In: R. J. Lax, S. Bach, & J. A.

Burland (Eds.), *Rapprochement*. New York: Jason Aronson.

McGilchrist, I. (2009). *The Master and His Emissary: The Divided Brain and the Making of the Western World*. New Haven, CT. Yale University Press.

Mollon, P. (1984). Shame in relation to narcissistic disturbance. *British Journal of Medical Psychology*, 57: 207–214.

Mollon, P. (1985). The non-mirroring mother and the missing paternal dimension in a case of narcissistic disturbance. *Psychoanalytic Psychotherapy*, 1: 35–47.

Mollon, P. (1986). Narcissistic vulnerability and the fragile self: a failure of mirroring. *British Journal of Medical Psychology*, 59: 317–324.

Mollon, P. (1993). *The Fragile Self. The Structure of Narcissistic Disturbance.* London: Whurr.

Mollon, P. (1996). *Multiple Selves, Multiple Voices: Working with Trauma, Violation, and Dissociation*. Chichester, UK: Wiley.

Mollon, P. (1998). *Remembering Trauma. A Clinician's Guide to Memory and Illusion*. Chichester, UK: Wiley.

Mollon, P. (2000). *Kohut's diagram of narcissistic disorder.* In: *Drawing the Soul*. London: Rathbone.

Mollon, P. (2001a). *Releasing the Self. The Healing Legacy of Heinz Kohut*. London: Whurr.

Mollon, P. (2001b). *Dark dimensions of multiple personality.* In: V. Sinason (Ed.), Attachment, Trauma and Multiplicity. London: Routledge.

Mollon, P. (2002). *Shame and Jealousy: The Hidden Turmoils*. London: Karnac.

Mollon, P. (2005a). The inherent shame of sexuality. *British Journal of Psychotherapy*, 22 (2): 167–177.

Mollon, P. (2005b). *EMDR and the Energy Therapies. Psychoanalytic Perspectives*. London: Karnac.

Mollon, P. (2008). *Psychoanalytic Energy Psychotherapy.* London: Karnac.

Mollon, P. (2011). A Kohutian perspective on the foreclosure of the Freudian transference in modern British technique.

References

Psychoanalytic Inquiry, 31(1): 28–41.

Mollon, P. (2014a). Revisiting "Analysis terminable and interminable" – expressions of death instinct by patients and
analysts. *Psychoanalytic Inquiry*, 34(1). Special Issue: Con-
tours of Analytic Time and Space: Interminable Treatments,
Extra- and Post-Analytic.

Mollon, P. (2014b). Attachment and energy psychology: Ex-
plorations at the interface of bodily, mental, relational, and
transpersonal aspects of human behaviour and experience. In:
K. White (Ed.), *Talking Bodies*. London: Karnac.

Mollon, P. (2015). *The Disintegrating Self: Psychotherapy of Adult
ADHD, Autistic Spectrum, and Somato-Psychic Conditions*.
London: Karnac.

Money-Kyrle, R. (1963). Megalomania. Paper presented to the
Imago Group, London, published in D. Meltzer (Ed.), *The
Collected Papers of Roger Money-Kyrle*. Strath Tay, UK: Clunie
Press, 1978.

Nobus, D. (2000). Why I am never myself. In: B. Seu (Ed.), *Who
Am I? The Ego and the Self in Psychoanalysis* (pp. 181–198).
London. Rebus.

Perelberg, R. J. (2003). Full and empty spaces in the analytic process. *International Journal of Psychoanalysis*, 84: 579–592.

Perelberg, R. J. (2004). Narcissistic configurations: Violence and its
absence in treatment. *International Journal of Psychoanalysis*,
85(5): 1065–1079.

Rapaport, D., Schafer, R., & Gill, M. M. (1945). *Diagnostic
Psychological Testing: The Theory, Statistical Evaluation, and
Diagnostic Application of a Battery of Tests*. Chicago, IL: Year
Book Publishers.

Robbins, L. L. (1956). The borderline case. *Journal of the American
Psychoanalytic Association*, 4: 550–562.

Rosenfeld, H. (1971). A clinical approach to the psychoanalytic
theory of the life and death instincts: an investigation of the
aggressive aspects of narcissism. *International Journal of Psychoanalysis*, 52: 169–178.

Rosenfeld, H. (1987). *Impasse and Interpretation: Therapeutic and Anti-therapeutic Factors in the Psychoanalytic Treatment of Psychotic, Borderline and Neurotic Patients.* London: Tavistock and the Institute of Psychoanalysis.

Schore, A. N. (1994). *Affect Regulation and the Origin of the Self.* Hillsdale, NJ: Lawrence Erlbaum.

Schucman, H. (1975). *A Course in Miracles.* Mill Valley, CA: Foundation for Inner Peace.

Shaw, D. (2013). *Traumatic Narcissism. Relational Systems of Subjugation.* New York: Routledge.

Solomon, M. F., Lang, J. A., & Grotstein, J. S. (1987). Clinical impressions of the borderline patient. In: J. S. Grotstein, M. F. Solomon, & J. A. Lang (Eds.), *The Borderline Patient. Emerging Concepts in Diagnosis, Psychodynamics, and Treatment.* Hillsdale, NJ: The Analytic Press.

Stark, E. (2007). *Coercive Control. How Men Entrap Women in Personal Relationships.* New York: Oxford University Press.

Stern, A. (1938). Psychoanalytic investigation of and therapy in the borderline group of neuroses. *Psychoanalytic Quarterly*, 7: 467–489.

Stoller, R. (1976). *Perversion. The Erotic Form of Hatred.* London: Harvester.

Strozier, C. (2001). *Heinz Kohut. The Making of a Psychoanalyst.* New York: Farrar, Straus and Giroux.

Tronick, E., Als, H., Adamson, L., Wise, S., & Brazelton, T. (1978). The infant's response to entrapment between contradictory messages in face to face interactions. *Journal of the American Academy of Child Psychiatry*, 17: 1–13.

Turco, R. N. (2014). Traumatic Narcissism: Relational Systems of Subjugation, by Daniel Shaw (Routledge, New York and London, 2013, 167 pp.). *Psychodynamic Psychiatry*, 42(4): 721–725.

Tweedy, R. (2013). *The God of the Left Hemisphere: Blake, Bolte Taylor and the Myth of Creation.* London: Routledge.

Vinge, L. (1967). *The Narcissus Theme in Western Literature up to the Early Nineteenth Century.* Lund, Sweden: Gleerups.

Walby, S., & Towers, J. (2018). Untangling the concept of coercive control: Theorizing domestic violent crime. *Criminology & Criminal Justice,* 18(1): 7–28. https://doi.org/10.1177/1748895817743541.

Walmsley-Johnson, H. (2018). *Look What You Made Me Do: A Powerful Memoir of Coercive Control.* London: Macmillan.

West, M. (2016). *Into the Darkest Places. Early Relational Trauma and Borderline States of Mind.* London: Karnac.

Williams, D. (1998). *Autism and Sensing: The Unlost Instinct.* London: Jessica Kingsley.

Wilshire, B. (1982). *Role Playing and Identity. The Limits of Theatre as Metaphor.* Bloomington, IN: Indiana University Press.

Winnicott, D. W. (1960). Ego distortion in terms of true and false self. In: *The Maturational Processes and the Facilitating Environment.* London: Hogarth.

Wolberg, A. R. (1982). *Psychoanalytic Psychotherapy of the Borderline Patient.* New York: Thieme-Stratton.

Zilboorg, G. (1941). Ambulatory schizophrenia. *Psychiatry,* 4: 149–155.

INDEX

Index